MARY McCARTHY

MODERN LITERATURE SERIES

GENERAL EDITOR: Philip Winsor

    (continued on last page of book)

MARY McCARTHY

Willene Schaefer Hardy

FREDERICK UNGAR PUBLISHING CO.
NEW YORK

For John Edward Hardy
and, in memory, Myrtle Pack Hall

Copyright © 1981 by Frederick Ungar Publishing Co., Inc.
Printed in the United States of America
Designed by Anita Duncan

Library of Congress Cataloging in Publication Data

Hardy, Willene Schaefer, 1937-
  Mary McCarthy.

  (Modern literature series)
  Bibilography: p.
  Includes index.
  1. McCarthy, Mary, 1912-
Criticism and interpretation.   I. Title.
II. Series: Modern literature monographs.
PS3525.A1435Z66   818'.5209   81-40462
ISBN 0-8044-2350-4   AACR2

Contents

Chronology

I

~.~.~.~.~.~.~.~.~.~.~.~.~.~.~.~.~.~.~.

Biography

Mary McCarthy's name became a household word with the publication of *The Group* in 1963. The popularity of the novel surprised her. She had not set out to write a best seller, in spite of the suspicions of some of her critics, and she did not follow *The Group* with an effort to capitalize on its success. It was eight years before her next novel came out, and *Birds of America* bears none of the markings of a product seeking a mass market. In the intervening years, McCarthy turned much of her attention to the war in Vietnam, hoping by her celebrity to attract a wide readership for her arguments against American involvement in that conflict. Throughout her career, she has been a serious novelist and essayist; the fame was something of a lucky accident. Previously, she had been known and appreciated by a fairly limited intellectual public, and so hostile to *The Group* were some of its members that Elaine Showalter writes, "with . . . critics like these, and best-sellerdom to boot, *The Group* virtually destroyed Mary McCarthy's literary and intellectual reputation."[1] McCarthy has, however, weathered that storm nicely. Tranquility is not her natural state, in any case; as Brock Brower observes, "she has easily survived as much scandal as she has published."[2]

Mary McCarthy was born in Seattle in June 1912, the first child and only daughter of Roy and Theresa

Preston McCarthy. Roy was the son of wealthy Minneapolis Irish Catholics, Theresa the daughter of a
prominent Seattle lawyer and his beautiful Jewish
wife. Both families had opposed the marriage because
of religious differences and because of Roy's health; he
had a bad heart and had been told that he might die at
any time. After the marriage, however, both families
contributed to the young McCarthys' support, particularly the older McCarthys.

Mary McCarthy remembers the first six years of
her life as idyllic, with "picnics . . . Easter egg hunts, a
succession of birthday cakes and ice-cream molds, a
glorious May basket . . . parties" and loving, indulgent
parents. That life was undoubtedly expensive. Desiring to have Roy and his family—there were four
children—nearby, where they could try to curb ex-
penditures, the older McCarthys decided to move
them to Minneapolis. In 1918, the six-year-old Mary,
her parents, and her three younger brothers traveled
by train from Seattle; by the time they arrived in
Minneapolis, all were ill with influenza.

Both parents died soon after their arrival. The
children became the charges of their paternal grandparents, who moved them to a house financially supported by the McCarthys and presided over by an
aunt and her husband in the tyranny described in
Memories of a Catholic Girlhood. During the five
years in Minneapolis, the young Mary found in her
Catholicism both escape from her wretched home and
direction for development.

In 1923, she was rescued from an unhappy life by
her maternal grandfather, who took her back to Seattle; there, life with him and her grandmother was, if
not normal, at least secure and ordered. For two years
Mary continued her Catholic education, but after failing to distinguish herself as a "superior" girl—as she
had done easily in the little school in Minneapolis—

and losing her faith, she transferred from the Catholic school to a public school, where, to the detriment of her grades, she discovered boys. Her grandfather was dissatisfied with that turn of events; and so, after only one year, she was sent to Annie Wright, an Episcopal boarding school in Tacoma, where she finished high school in 1929.

During the summer after graduation, McCarthy attended acting classes in Seattle and there met Harold Johnsrud, who was to become her first husband. In the fall of that year, she went east to Vassar, where she studied English literature and the classics. She was graduated four years later and immediately married Johnsrud. They settled in New York, where he attempted to establish himself in the theater, and McCarthy, her own ambition to be an actress quelled at least in part by her husband's negative opinion of her talent, began to publish book reviews in *The Nation* and *The New Republic*. In 1935, she collaborated with Margaret Marshall on a series of articles attacking the literary critics, among them Joseph Wood Krutch, Henry Seidel Canby, and John Chamberlain. Among the few who received words of praise was Edmund Wilson, who was to become McCarthy's second husband. Mary McCarthy early made it clear that, whatever might be her place in American letters, it would not be as an echo of the literary establishment.

During these years she was associated with left-wing intellectuals. She never joined the Communist Party, but she had friends who did. Her essay "My Confession" (included in *On the Contrary*) is a political autobiography which tells how, by "accident," she offended the Stalinists by becoming a Trotskyite before the mainstream leftists had become disenchanted with Stalin. At a party, the novelist James T. Farrell asked McCarthy whether she thought Trotsky was entitled to a hearing; out of political ignorance and be-

wilderment that anyone might consider him *not* entitled to a hearing, she answered yes and soon saw her
name on the letterhead of the Committee for the Defense of Leon Trotsky.

In 1936, she was divorced from Johnsrud. In
1936–37, she worked for Covici-Friede, a left-wing
publishing house. In 1937, largely because of her affair
with Philip Rahv, she was made drama editor of the
newly revived *Partisan Review*. She confesses that the
importance of the position was slight. It was believed
that since McCarthy had been married to an actor, she
knew something about the theater, but in any event,
drama was not a significant subject to the editors of
the magazine, and she could do no harm.

McCarthy has always attracted attention. It is a
cliché of the moment to say that this or that celebrity
is a very "private person," but the phrase is not likely
to be applied to Mary McCarthy. Brower quotes an
unnamed "disgruntled listener" who once objected,
"Why is everybody always talking about her? Do you
know I once knew more about Mary McCarthy and
Philip Rahv than I knew about *myself*?"[3] Her life is
an open book, or part of many books: she says what
she means and tells what she does, in interviews, in
essays, and in fiction, no matter who is offended, and
in the course of the years, many people have been.

The essays for the *Partisan Review* are interesting
for their precise and often cutting style and for their
iconoclasm. A mature McCarthy looking back at these
early reviews finds their superior manner irritating but
does not take issue with their content. It is fair to
point out that the 1930s were hardly the Golden Age
of American theater; many of the plays condemned
by the youthful critic have earned obscurity since
then, and her qualified favorable responses—to *Our
Town*, for example—have also been vindicated by the
passage of time. Her judgments, however, were so

severe that Edmund Wilson told her that she did not so much review a play as "draw up a crushing brief against it."[4]

Wilson became McCarthy's second husband in 1938; he was the father of her only child, Reuel. It was a stormy marriage, of which glimpses appear in the fiction, especially in *A Charmed Life*. Perhaps McCarthy would have begun to write fiction sooner or later—although she had been discouraged at Vassar by being told that she had a critical rather than a creative mind—but to Wilson she owes at least the moment and manner of beginning:

After we'd been married for about a week, he said, "I think you have a talent for writing fiction." And he put me in a little room. He didn't literally lock the door, but he said "Stay in there!" And I did. I just sat down, and it just came. It was the first story I had ever written, really: the first story in *The Company She Keeps*.[5]

Robert Penn Warren published the story in the Spring issue of the *Southern Review*, 1939. The career had taken a new and promising direction.

The Company She Keeps, a group of stories unified by a heroine in search of herself, came out in 1942. The volume contains the infamous and excellent "The Man in the Brooks Brothers Shirt."

"Lots of women had taken up with a man on the train before—or at least they'd *thought* about doing it—but this was the first time anybody ever *wrote* about it," recalls Miss [Elizabeth] Hardwick. "I was absolutely bowled over by it."[6]

From the distance of the eighties, it is hard to remember when candor about sex was not only avant-garde but downright shocking, especially by a woman writer. In her fiction as in her criticism, McCarthy turned out to be devastatingly honest, and not just about sex. Her heroine is not always shown in the most

flattering light, nor is the company she keeps. The
Yale man, for example, is reportedly based on an intellectual of McCarthy's acquaintance, but she used John
Chamberlain, she says, as "just a kind of good-looking
clothes-hanger," the basis for a portrait of a morally
compromised liberal who is really a "broad type."[7]

In 1945, McCarthy and Wilson were separated,
and during the 1945–46 school year she taught at
Bard. "I liked teaching because I loved this business of
studying," she said of the experience; but two years
later, in 1948, she did not enjoy Sarah Lawrence during her one term there because the students were not
very good.

In 1946, McCarthy traveled in Italy with Bowden
Broadwater, a writer and teacher, and in December of
that year she married him. After living in New York,
Vermont, and Rhode Island, they bought a house in
Wellfleet, Massachusetts, in 1952, establishing themselves not far from where Edmund Wilson and his
new wife lived, a situation McCarthy draws from in *A
Charmed Life*. During the late forties, her associations
with the Europe-America Groups—organized to raise
money for European intellectuals—provided her with
materials for *The Oasis*, a utopian book which she
calls a *conte philosophique*.

During the fifties, McCarthy traveled a good deal
—to Portugal, for example, for *The New Yorker*—
and her life fell into a pattern of alternating periods
alone in Europe writing with periods in Vermont or
New York with Broadwater and Reuel.[8] The marriage had been failing for some time when, in 1959, on
a tour for the State Department, she met the diplomat
James West in Poland. In 1961, after an Alabama divorce from Broadwater, she married West.

By this time, McCarthy had produced a considerable body of work, including, besides the titles already
mentioned, two books of art history, *Venice Observed*

and *The Stones of Florence*; an academic novel, *The Groves of Academe*; an autobiography, *Memories of a Catholic Girlhood*; a collection of the drama criticism, *Sights and Spectacles: 1937–1956;* and a volume of stories and sketches, *Cast a Cold Eye.* After she and West settled in Paris, she collected and published again, with additions, the early theater pieces. But more importantly, during the same year, 1963, she published *The Group.*

She was already an established writer. *The Oasis* had won the *Horizon* prize, and she had had two Guggenheim Fellowships. She had been much talked about and often admired among the literati, but now she delighted many and outraged some by writing a book that everybody read. It is different from anything else she or any other novelist had done before, this mock chronicle of eight Vassar women in the seven years after their graduation in 1933. It is an accurate and detailed examination of an era's education and expectations, fashions and follies; it concludes that nothing much came of all that promise. The book made her "internationally famous," Doris Grumbach writes, "as only a popular novelist in our time becomes famous."[9] Its reputation was enlarged, if not enhanced, three years later by the appearance of a lavish movie bearing its title but otherwise little related to the novel.

The book that everybody read and "everyone of importance"[10] reviewed was widely condemned by critics as too detailed, as trivial, as sensational. It was a matter of no great importance to the majority of readers who had never met McCarthy, but the materials of *The Group* were drawn from her own experience, and the characters, in part, from people whom she had known, including her Vassar classmates. Grumbach reports that one horrified alumna wanted McCarthy's degree rescinded for this "catalogue of venery, a disgrace to the printed word, and a blight on the reputation of a fine institution."[11] One supposes that she was referring to the account of Dottie's brief affair, published separately as a "much scandalmongered 1954 story" which, according to Brower, "does for contraception what *Moby Dick* did for whaling."[12] Dottie's struggles with her diaphragm, however, are funny, and so is her seduction. Mary McCarthy is as irreverent about sex as about other human practices.

McCarthy wrote that during the thirties she was politically "unserious," and the phrase has attached itself to her like the "cold eye" of the title taken from Yeats; both descriptions have been applied indiscriminately, particularly the former. The "accident" by which she became anti-Stalinist might have produced a different response in a different moral sensibility. McCarthy has not often been an activist, but her essays on (Senator Joseph) McCarthyism are surely as serious as anything written on the subject, which is distinctly political. In the sixties, she became passionately involved in the effort to end American involvement in Vietnam. Her reason was moral. Desiring firsthand knowledge, she made separate trips to South Vietnam and North Vietnam, and her findings are reported in *Vietnam* and *Hanoi*.

As McCarthy's fiction makes clear, she believes in putting up a stake where moral questions are involved. That is partly why she and West bought a house in Castine, Maine, in 1967: "if I was going to take a stand against U.S. policy, I ought to have a piece of U.S. ground under my feet." More dramatic, however, was the personal risk involved in traveling to Hanoi, where American bombs were falling. In the autobiographical introduction to *The Seventeenth Degree* (containing the Vietnam materials republished in a single volume), she muses, "That word 'witness' I was using so freely was the same as 'martyr' in Greek. Did I want to be a martyr? I don't know."

During the seventies, McCarthy published *The Writing on the Wall, and Other Literary Essays.* She viewed the Watergate hearings with a novelist's eye, and published her impressions as *The Mask of State.* At the beginning and end of the decade she published novels, *Birds of America* in 1971 and *Cannibals and Missionaries* in 1979. Both novels have international settings, with only their beginnings in America; as an expatriate, McCarthy does not feel that she can write accurately about Americans in America. In 1980, she brought out a volume of lectures, *Ideas and the Novel.* She and West still live in Paris and spend part of each summer in the house in Maine.

McCarthy belongs to a privileged class. She knew poverty as a child, but it was a special, artificial kind of poverty—a deprivation of beauty and an assault on her pride. Harrowing as it was, it was not common poverty; even as she suffered the humiliations inflicted on her by her guardians, she felt superior to them. She has made a lot of money, and she likes to spend money; she is free in a way that most people are not, and she is aware of that fact. Her fiction is about her own class, and her characters are privileged, too; they are formally educated, and though they may work hard, their labors are of the humane sorts which enhance life: they write, they paint, they teach, they are in politics. But as McCarthy is fond of remarking, from each according to his abilities; she is very demanding, and she finds that people too often take life as they find it, comfortable and limited, without examining it or themselves very closely.

She is sometimes a satirist in an age which does not respond well to satire, more often a comic writer in an age which does not see much to laugh about. She

writes for the predominantly liberal intellectuals of
our time, and she writes *about* them. She holds the
mirror up to life at such an angle that the reader
catches a glimpse of himself, not quite distorted but
perhaps—ever so slightly—exaggerated.

2.

~.~.~.~.~.~.~.~.~.~.~.~.~.~.~.~.~.~.~.

Memories of a Catholic Girlhood:
The Author's Early Years

People who have read *Memories of a Catholic Girl-hood* do not forget it. Mary McCarthy speaks of the "pristine, fairy-tale period," the first six idyllic years in Seattle with her parents; later events in Minneapolis evoke the dark side of the fairy tale. The little princess and princes fell into the hands of two wicked step-parents and remained in their power for five crucial years. The story is worthy of the Brothers Grimm; it is often labeled Dickensian, and that description, too, is apt. In *The Company She Keeps*, McCarthy gives Margaret Sargent a similar life history, and Margaret is highly critical of "this degenerated Victorian novel." Like her creator, she knows what it is to have a "sense of artistic decorum that like a hoity-toity wife [is] continually showing one's poor biography the door."

Memories of a Catholic Girlhood is in the form of eight personal narrative-essays, or memoirs, most of them originally published in *The New Yorker*. A prefatory essay, "To the Reader," summarizes Mc-Carthy's family history and early childhood, and details the benefits of a Catholic education from the point of view of one who lost her faith at twelve and never recovered it. The memoirs that constitute the book's chapters are linked by commentaries which offer fur-ther reflection or new information, or explain the slight extent to which the materials are fictionalized.

These commentaries in particular show a desire to locate the truth, to solve the mysteries of a childhood
that neither McCarthy nor her brothers have been able
to understand.

She writes that her family were "ordinary people
who behaved quite oddly, to each other and to us four
children, [and] that, I think, is the source of the fas-
cination. One wants . . . to learn either that they were
not ordinary of that their behavior was not as odd as it
looked." The idyllic years were in their way almost as
odd as the Dickensian years. After her marriage to
Roy McCarthy, Theresa Preston, daughter of a Jewish
mother and a Protestant father, converted to Catholicism; and she taught her children that it was "a special
treat to be a Catholic." But virtually everything the
children remembered about their early life was a special treat. Perhaps their memories were heightened by
the contrast to Minneapolis, but certainly the children
were pampered and cherished by their doomed parents. The girl remembers "little diamond rings" and an
ermine muff and neckpiece. Her mother was beautiful,
her father handsome and dashing and surrounded by a
"romantic aura." Because of his bad heart, he often lay
in bed, but while he was there, he planned "treats and
surprises." He maintained a law office, but the young
family were supported chiefly by the McCarthys,
whose decision it was for them to move to Minneapolis.

The trip from Seattle to Minneapolis in 1918
brought an end to treats. When, on the train, the entire family came down with influenza, the children
"did not understand whether the chattering of [their]
teeth and Mama's lying torpid in the berth were not
somehow part of the trip." In Minneapolis, met by
"stretchers, a wheel chair, redcaps, distraught offi-
cials," they were certain that the illness was the "beginning of a delightful holiday."

They woke from their fevers in the "bleak, shabby, utilitarian" sewing room of their grandparents' splendid house. In the care of strangers, without being told, they "came to know" that their parents were dead and that their own condition had changed abruptly. In the epilogue to the first memoir, "Yonder Peasant, Who Is He?," McCarthy writes that "we orphan children . . . were treated as if . . . being orphans were a crime we had committed," adding, "Read *poor* for *orphan* throughout and you get a kind of allegory or broad social satire on the theme of wealth and poverty."

Desiring to keep the children together and away from "the Protestants," the McCarthy grandparents purchased a house two blocks from their own and there installed the children in the charge of their great-aunt Margaret and her new husband, Myers Shriver. During the years 1918–23, the McCarthys paid a good deal of money for the support of that household, but life there was so wretched that Mary and Kevin, the oldest of her brothers, occasionally ran away—separately, for the children were not close friends—hoping to find an orphanage, a sanctuary to which they felt entitled. After each such episode, the runaway was returned to the McCarthy house to enjoy a brief, luxurious vacation—sleeping, however, in the sewing room—before being sent back to the dreary house on Blaisdell Avenue. The grandparents did not visit that house or respond to the many evidences of the children's poverty and lovelessness. If the style of living which Myers and Margaret purchased with the ample allowance reeked unnecessarily of poverty, it was no doubt practical to overlook that fact. These dutiful relatives agreed, in any event, that it was desirable to attempt to undo the damage done by the parents in "spoiling" the children.

Cakes and picnics were the stuff of a dreamlike

past; Aunt Margaret fed the children a healthful diet of "lumpy mush and watery boiled potatoes," turnips and parsnips and other root vegetables. "Everything fibrous, tenacious, watery, and knobby in the Irish peasant stock" expressed itself in their diet. (Uncle Myers had different meals, however.) Transplanted from the mild Seattle climate, the children were forced outdoors to play for hours in the bitter Minneapolis winter, their deprivation apparent even in the shabbiness of their clothing.

More fundamental to the children's unhappiness than the austerity of their food and clothing was the character of their guardians. Although Aunt Margaret seems to have been motivated by a sense of duty, Uncle Myers, to whom she always deferred, apparently had a streak of tyranny in his nature. Two events in the second memoir, "A Tin Butterfly," testify to his meanspiritedness. On one occasion, he furiously beat Mary after she had won an essay contest at school, "to teach [her] a lesson, he said, lest [she] become stuck-up." On another, he and Margaret alternately beat Mary in an unsuccessful effort to force a false confession that she had stolen a tin butterfly belonging to her youngest brother. The truth about the tin butterfly remains a mystery, but the incident sums up the penury and injustice which ruled the children's lives. Uncle Myers frequently ate Cracker Jack, and on one occasion he gave Sheridan, the youngest child and the only one for whom he showed any tenderness, a box for himself. The prize inside was the tin butterfly. The children were virtually possessionless—gifts from the Seattle grandparents were put away to be "kept" because they were "too good" to be used—and Sheridan was inordinately fond of the worthless toy. After about a week, it disappeared and was the object of a frantic search; it reappeared, inexplicably, under the tablecloth at Mary's place at table. For that reason, illogically, she was suspected of having stolen it.

There was a kind of class antipathy between the children and their aunt's coarse husband. Little was known of his past, and, McCarthy writes, he "had to contend with Irish social snobbery, which looked upon him dispassionately from four sets of green eyes and set him down as 'not a gentleman.' " Perhaps his determination to keep from the young Mary anything that was "too good" for her, his readiness to ridicule anything that to his mind appeared affected, was in part his revenge against the Irish Catholics in Minneapolis for their suspicion of "all the northern bloods and their hateful Lutheran heresy." In any case, it was her Catholicism, McCarthy believes, that saved her during those years with the Shrivers; if Myers thought it was her escape from him, he was right.

Poor and *"ugly"* as it no doubt was, from a larger perspective, the little parish church was the young Mary's *"equivalent of Gothic cathedrals and illuminated manuscripts and mystery plays"*; and in the little parochial school, she could excel without being ridiculed. She became *"the best runner . . . the best actress and elocutionist and the second most devout"* in the school, and she stood at the head of her class. In "To the Reader," McCarthy comments that *"no doubt"* the standards of the school *"were not very high, and they gave me a false idea of myself; I have never excelled at athletics elsewhere. Nor have I ever been devout again. When I left the competitive atmosphere of the parochial school, my religion withered on the stalk."* The benefits of a Catholic education, however, were permanent: an exposure to the Latin language; an acquaintance with the saints, and with them some knowledge of world history and the history of ideas, enlivened by *"violent partisanship"*; the passionate identification with *"a losing cause . . . a kind of strain-*

ing against reality that . . . is rare in America, where
children are instructed in the virtues of the system
they live under"; the conception of *"something prior*
to and beyond utility" in education, *"an idea of sheer*
wastefulness."

This "wastefulness" McCarthy associates with her
father and the "wildness" in his and her own nature
which she attributes to the Catholic side of her ances-
try. But the McCarthy romanticism was balanced by
the classical legacy of her Preston grandfather, also a
lawyer and the "most virtuous person I knew." It was
he who rescued Mary from the Shrivers.

"A Tin Butterfly" ends with his visit to Minneapolis, at the end of which he took Mary home with
him to Seattle. The boys remained in the charge of the
McCarthys, an instance of injustice permitted by a just
man that McCarthy has never understood, although
she admits that at the time it did not bother her. The
boys were sent away to school, however; only Sheridan, Myers's favorite, remained with the Shrivers until
he too was old enough to go. Effectively the little
tyranny was dissolved, and within five years both the
Shrivers were dead.

During the Minneapolis years, Eleanor Widmer
says, Catholicism was Mary McCarthy's "one source
of elitism"[1]; and she broke with it soon after moving
to Seattle. There is more truth than justice in the observation; it is common for adolescents to lose the
faith of their childhood. In Seattle, Mary was enrolled
for two years in a convent school. Three of the
memoirs are of her seventh- and eighth-grade experiences at Forest Ridge. "The Blackguard" describes her
"intense theological anxiety" on behalf of her grandfather, a baptized Protestant. It was relieved only
when one of the nuns found doctrinal evidence that he
was not irretrievably damned. The grandfather in
question knew nothing of this agitation on behalf of

his soul. He maintained a respectful friendship with the headmistress until one of the sisters compared Mary to Lord Byron, "brilliant but unsound." Mr. Preston did not share his granddaughter's delight; he protested to the headmistress against this association of his "innocent granddaughter with that degenerate blackguard, Byron," and a retraction resulted.

The other two chapters about the Forest Ridge experiences are "*C'est le Premier Pas Qui Coûte*" and "Names." As an outsider, Mary was unable to attract the notice of the "superior girls" in the new school. Finally, in a dramatic move, she commanded the awed attention of the entire school by announcing that she had lost her faith; secretly she planned to regain it "in time for Wednesday confessions" so that her soul would be in jeopardy for only four days. After marshaling an assortment of doubts for presentation to the priests and listening to their patient assurances, Mary realized that she had indeed lost her faith. With the entire convent in a state of "uneasiness," she tried to feel faith "as a public duty." Her simulated return to the fold was, finally, as much as her straying had been, a way of controlling the social order.

"Names" tells of the mysterious nickname "Cye," the meaning of which she never learned; and of the misunderstanding by which, having stained her sheets with blood from a cut, Mary was unable to make the nuns believe that she had not "become a woman." Already pretending to be a Catholic, she now had to pretend that she menstruated because the nuns were certain that she was too embarrassed to admit the truth (they issued her supplies every month). She had become "a walking mass of lies," even answering to the hated nickname with feigned good humor. She left the false identity behind when she went to public school for the ninth grade. Finally, at Annie Wright Seminary in Tacoma, where she spent the last three

years of high school, she distinguished herself academ-
ically and became a "big shot" as well.

"The Figures in the Clock" tells of Mary's tri-
umphant performance in the senior play as the rebel
Catiline, the "damned soul, proud and unassimilable,
the marked, gifted man." To her mind, "Catiline was
not only a hero—he was me." Still, her main speech—
from Sallust, delivered in the "buckram translation" of
the Latin teacher, Miss Gowrie—repeated night after
night in rehearsal, "awakened a tiny doubt: Was the
Catiline I admired so much merely a vulgar arsonist, as
Cicero and his devotees contended?"

The shared experience of the play—Miss Gowrie
wrote it and directed its tremendously successful
presentation—was the foundation of a friendship between the young actress and the austere middle-aged
Scotswoman who was not a favorite of the other girls.
"It was the whim of oddity, doubtless, that first decided me to 'like' Miss Gowrie." Self-conscious and
superior, the young Mary did not reflect that her "discovery of Miss Gowrie was disclosing . . . certain
strange landscapes" in herself. Under Miss Gowrie's
tutelage, she "fell in love with Caesar." She sees the
event as the awakening of her Preston blood.

Caesar, of course, was my grandfather: just, laconic, severe,
magnanimous, detached. . . . Catiline was my McCarthy
ancestors—the wild streak in my heredity, the wreckers on
the Nova Scotia coast. To my surprise, I chose Caesar and
the rule of law. This does not mean that the seesaw between these two opposed forces terminated; one might say,
in fact, that it only began during my last years in the Seminary when I recognized the beauty of an ablative absolute
and of a rigorous code of conduct.

But Miss Gowrie felt it was her duty to report
her "favorites" for violations of school rules. Mary
McCarthy's duty was to "break the rules and take all
offered risks, in order not to graduate in an orderly,

commonplace fashion." During the last week of school
Miss Gowrie caught Mary coming through the gym
window on her way back from meeting a boy—"the
only crime that was considered serious by the principal." In the resultant interview, Mary came to understand that the principal did not want the truth:

I was the top student in my class, and the school, I perceived, was counting on me to do it credit in my college
boards . . . the lie was a favor being asked of me, not only
for my own sake and the school's but on behalf of poor,
misguided Miss Gowrie, who ought to have known better
than to prowl about at night in her bathrobe in the last
week of school.

The principal avoided asking Mary what she had been
doing; Mary volunteered the half-truth that she had
gone out to smoke, a lesser offense than meeting a
boy.

A different phase of Mary's growing up is detailed in "Yellowstone Park." At Annie Wright, Mary
had managed to make friends with older girls by pretending to be more experienced than she was. The
summer before her junior year, she was invited by
Ruth and Betty Bent to go home with them for a
three-week visit in Medicine Springs, Montana. Although at school she wrote stories "about prostitutes
with 'eyes like dirty dishwater,' " to her deep shame
her grandparents regarded her as too young to travel
alone or go out with boys. The Bent girls had promised "plenty of dates," a lively crowd, and complete
freedom, but these attractions would not win her
grandparents' consent to the trip. Yellowstone Park,
on the other hand, would.

It was too bad, I remarked casually, in . . . my last school
letter home, that the trip was out of the question: the girls
had been planning to take me on a tour of Yellowstone
Park. That was all that was needed. It was as simple as

selling him a renewal of his subscription to the *National Geographic*.

Medicine Springs, it turned out, was nowhere near Yellowstone; it was "a small, flat, yellowish town set in the middle of nowhere." Arriving at the Bents' house, Mary was taken aback by their unceremonious style. "If the Bents had been poor, I would not have felt so ill-at-ease and indeed paralyzed," but she knew them not to be poor. Yet the house was without ornament or distinction, and Mrs. Bent had no apparent function other than answering the telephone and ironing the girls' dresses.

But Ruth and Betty were talking of a dance and dates, and Mary took heart, imagining "smooth, sleek boys" in "white linen suits," a "long piazza, a barbecue pit, and silver flasks glinting in the moonlight." But there were no boys in Medicine Springs, and all the men were marrried except for Betty's date. Mary's first real date was with a married man whose wife was away—"the handsomest man in Medicine Springs and very hard to please." Mary recognized him as "common" but decided that "from a distance he could pass." In any case, she was in no position to withdraw from the proceedings. The three girls and their dates set out in three cars; periodically all three stopped, out in the country, and a bottle of the "very best" moonshine was passed around. Mary found it undrinkable until she discovered that she could hold a mouthful and gradually work it down. She could not, of course, talk. "Bob Berdan sang, and I rode along tight-lipped beside him, with a mouth full of unswallowed moonshine, which washed around my teeth as the car bumped along the rutted road." The dance, finally arrived at, was in "a sort of shed" and was attended by "rough-looking, unshaven, coatless men pushing and grabbing and yelling while an old woman played the piano."

Some hours later, McCarthy writes, she woke in a strange room in bed with Bob Berdan. "As I lay there, grimly taking stock, he woke up and his arm tightened; he started muttering tenderly. Men, I had heard, were like that after. . . . I was too horror-stricken to finish the thought." But nothing had happened; the girls had taken Mary's dress to clean it because she had gotten sick, Bob explained, and he "would never take advantage of a sweet kid" like her.

Traveling home alone on the train, Mary took up with a party of tourists—two men and two women— just out of Yellowstone. She hoped to find out enough about the park from them to present a convincing report to her grandfather, but they lacked "the grasp of detail" which he "expected from a narrative." A fatherly conductor warned her that these people were bad company: "They changed berths," he told her. "A month before I might have argued the issue. . . . But now I did not have the heart to go against his instructions. It would crush him if he caught me talking to them. . . ." Regarding it also as "rather mean" to drop her new friends, Mary found herself

caught in a dilemma that was new to me then but which since has become horribly familiar: the trap of adult life, in which you are held, wriggling, powerless to act because you can see both sides. On that occasion, as generally in the future, I compromised. That is, I steered a zigzag course between the conductor and the two couples. . . . This jerky behavior, and the copious, dazzling smiles with which I tried to mitigate it, must have made both parties think I was deranged.

The final memoir, "Ask Me No Questions," is a life-sized sketch of Augusta Morganstern Preston, Mary McCarthy's Jewish maternal grandmother. Im-

posing, vain, and kindly, she "outlived them all." This
essay is McCarthy's first study of this grandmother,
and she approaches the subject with hesitation. For
forty years Mrs. Preston, once known as the most
beautiful woman in Seattle, refused to be photo-
graphed, and out of respect for her privacy her grand-
daughter refrained, during her life, from taking a
verbal likeness.

She figured in McCarthy's earliest memories and
survived well into her adulthood. But when she died,
the only mystery that her long life had solved was the
question of her hair, "black as a raven's wing"; she was
over eighty when the first sprinkling of white proved
that she had not dyed it—"Who ever saw natural hair
that color?"—but none of her "calumniators" lived to
concede the point. The story of her life was known
"in a general way" only; even her age was a secret,
though "we all knew, in a general way, calculating
from our own ages and from the laws of Nature, that
she had to be over eighty."

From the earliest years, before Minneapolis, Mc-
Carthy recalls her grandmother in an electric car,
wearing a suit and a veiled hat. She remembers an
attempt to organize the young McCarthy family's
bathroom so that each member would have a personal
towel: "I was impressed by this arrangement, which
seemed to me very stylish." But Roy McCarthy
failed to honor the system, and for "the first (and, I
think, the only) time I felt critical of my debonair
father, for I knew the strange lady would be cross
with him if she could see our bathroom now." The
"strange lady," unlike the "real" grandmother, did not
have white hair, do embroidery or tapestry, or "stare"
at the children over her glasses.

McCarthy's Jewish great-grandfather was a forty-
niner, but Augusta Morganstern offered no more information about him than that he had been a "broker"

in San Francisco. Reticent or unknowing, she would say, "half grumpily," to her questioning grand-daughter: "Why do you keep asking me all those old things?" Both her sisters married Jews. About her grandmother's attitude toward her Jewishness, or its effect on her, McCarthy has no clue. Whether the decision to marry a Gentile was an agonizing one, she could never discover. The only answer she would give to the question of why she chose Mr. Preston was that she "thought he would be good to her."

She was a gifted storyteller, however, and from one point of view "her entire married life was a suc-cession of comic anecdotes, of which she was both butt and heroine." In her stories "forever discon-certed, put out of countenance, dumbstruck," in real-ity she "was the disconcerting one, short of speech when she was not telling a story . . . impressive, forbid-ding." Her large, fine house was characteristically si-lent; much of every day she spent in her own rooms, preparing herself for the daily shopping trip which was the central activity of her life. She did not enter-tain, nor did the two young members of the family (her son, five years older than Mary, still lived at home). Occasionally their young friends visited, but they were never invited for a meal. Once a year, or possibly every two years, McCarthy writes, her grand-mother gave a catered tea.

Seeking an explanation for this "ungraciousness," McCarthy finds none adequate to account for the years of withdrawal. There was the early death of her daughter; there was a disastrous face-lift in 1916 or 1917, which explains the tight dotted veils which she wore in McCarthy's earliest memories, although the "not especially noticeable" scars are an unsatisfactory explanation for her reclusive life at sixty. McCarthy heard the event referred to as her grandmother's "tragedy," and she adds, "I will not query the appropriateness of the term. . . . It was a tragedy, for her, for her husband and family, who, deprived of her beauty through an act of folly, came to live in silence, like a house accursed."

"Ask Me No Questions" is an appropriate conclusion for the book, which has posited the oddness and mysteriousness of its subject. Augusta Preston knew Mary McCarthy from the beginning and might have told her something about herself and her relatives to help McCarthy understand her childhood. But she was as mysterious as any of the others.

Memories of a Catholic Girlhood is a collection; the introduction and commentaries do not make it a unified whole. There is a good deal of overlapping and backtracking, and what unity the book has lies in the developing and consistent personality of its author-subject and in the recurrent themes: education and religion as avenues to moral superiority which is tenuous at best, illusory at worst; the peculiar, inexplicable injustices of human beings; the recalcitrant nature of the real in conflict with the ideal; and the necessity of compromise.

Still, it is one of the most remarkable autobiographies in the English language. It has the best qualities of McCarthy's fiction. It is readable, written in a free-flowing, vital, always correct style. Its people are real, its scenes vivid, its pathos wryly qualified. It is richly and memorably detailed, and that is the chief source of its power. We retain the image of Lizzie McCarthy in her sun parlor, working on her tapestries, benevolently remote from the quaint orphaned grandchildren who exclaim over her good food and warm bathrooms before being returned to their dark box of a house on Blaisdell; of Mr. Preston, indignant at last when he learns that Mary is being punished for breaking her glasses by having to go without, going "straight as a

writ" up the McCarthy's front walk to settle the matter of the children; of Mary, declaiming in her splendid Catiline costume, or bumping along a country road
with a mouthful of moonshine; of Augusta Morganstern Preston, making a progress through a department store, or, with dainty greed, eating a bowlful of
apricots at home. We know the floor plan of the
Blaisdell house and the contents of Mr. Preston's dressing room. We even know about the cookbook of the
Ladies' Auxiliary of the Temple de Hirsch: Aunt
Rosie contributed recipes for chicken with noodles,
hamburger in tomatoes, and rhubarb pie, and Aunt
Eva one that begins, "Take a nice pair of sweetbreads,
add a cup of butter, a glass of good cream, sherry, and
some *foie gras*."

A striking thing about *Memories of a Catholic
Girlhood* is its detachment. It was denounced by one
reviewer as a "cry-baby" book, but that is precisely
what it is not. An abused or neglected child is in nature a pathetic spectacle, and the materials with which
McCarthy works are the stuff of tear-jerkers. But
when, for example, the child realizes that her parents
are dead, we are held at a distance from sentiment:

I considered myself clever to have guessed the truth about
my parents, like a child who proudly discovers that there
is no Santa Claus, but I would not speak of that knowledge
or even react to it privately, for I wished to have nothing
to do with it; I would not co-operate in this loss.

To be sure, in "Yonder Peasant, Who Is He?" the
images of scarecrow arms, raw hands, and "elderly
faces" are overdrawn; but then, we are invited to read
the chapter as allegory, as "an angry indictment of
privilege for its treatment of the underprivileged," an
outburst against the "McCarthy reasoning" by which,

"clearly, it was a generous impulse that kept us in the family at all." It is a general statement of the problem that McCarthy has in understanding her relatives and all the others who felt that

> my grandfather, a rich man, had behaved with extraordinary munificence in allotting a sum of money for our support and installing us with some disagreeable middle-aged relations in a dingy house two blocks distant from his own. . . . it was felt . . . that we led a privileged existence, privileged because we had no rights.

The point of this first memoir is the contrast between the luxury in which the grandparents lived and the poverty which they considered appropriate for the children.

It is an emotional chapter, but the dominant feeling is anger against injustice, not pity for the children. The other chapters are cooler. About herself McCarthy is as honest as she is about her relatives. Certainly she was in a more defensible position than were her guardians, but there is no sentimentalizing of the child's sensitivity or innocence. The essay that won her twenty-five dollars—the money was taken to "keep" for her, and that was the last she knew of it—and a furious beating is, for example, no evidence that the now-successful writer lisped in numbers. From frankly "cribbed" facts, she wrote the essay on "The Irish in American History"

> on the assumption that anybody who was Catholic must be Irish and . . . I went over the signers of the Declaration of Independence and added any name that sounded Irish. . . . All this was clothed in rhetoric invoking "the lilies of France"—God knows why, except that I was in love with France and somehow, through Marshal MacMahon, had made Lafayette out an Irishman. I believe that even Kosciusko figured as an Irishman *de coeur.*

On the occasion of the beating over the tin butterfly, Mary, who had been most heinously abused, "rejoiced" in the moral victory over Myers and Margaret as she "limped up to bed, with a crazy sense of inner victory," but the author observes unsympathetically, "It did not occur to me that I had been unchristian in refusing to answer a plea from Aunt Margaret's heart and conscience." The "cold eye" is not much warmer cast upon herself as a child than when it is cast upon her other subjects.

Throughout her childhood McCarthy was role playing, as children do, much of the time. Deprived of parents—for whom she might have played quite other roles, or none at all—she looked to the church, to her teachers, to her classmates, for an audience and attempted to win their esteem and her own by being the devout child, the excellent student, the superior girl. Later, in "Yellowstone Park," she played the young sophisticate, more doggedly than successfully. Very early, she worried about the impurity of her motives. After taking her first Communion in a state of sin— she had carelessly taken a sip of water that morning— she felt that she knew herself, and "*such dry self-knowledge is terrible.*" She had damned herself by choosing to "*preserve outward appearances*," to live up to the expectations of others. Yet the decision served the public need. That it is very difficult to do the right thing for the right reason is a major theme in the life and works of McCarthy.

Memories of a Catholic Girlhood shares several preoccupations with McCarthy's fiction. As we recognize the common concerns—the problems of the outsider; the peculiar effect of having had a childhood inconsistent with what one has become; the offensiveness of the tasteless, the common, the cheap; the desire to be superior; the value of traditions, including edu-

cation and religion and even fine linens—we realize
that Margaret Sargent, Martha Sinnott, and Rosamund
Brown are roles that Mary McCarthy, who wanted to
be an actress, could play very well. The heroines of
the novels are very close relatives of the girl in the
autobiography.

3

~~~~~~

"Preserve Me in Disunity:"
the Quest for Identity in
The Company She Keeps

Margaret Sargent is a fictional heroine whose story
was published fifteen years earlier than McCarthy's
autobiography, but she could easily be the girl of
Memories of a Catholic Girlhood a few years older
and a good deal more experienced. Like *Memories*,
The Company She Keeps is a collection of stories published separately before being brought together in a
book. Margaret's circumstances parallel McCarthy's
during the thirties. She has finished college and lives in
New York City; she marries young, and her first marriage ends in divorce. She reads manuscripts for a
publisher and writes for a liberal magazine. She is not
precisely Mary McCarthy, however, for she is from
Portland, Oregon, not Seattle, and the bizarre childhood which she recalls for her analyst was dominated
by an Aunt Clara who combines qualities of the Shrivers and the elder McCarthys.

Most writers use materials from their lives to
some extent, but McCarthy does less than most to disguise the fact in her fiction. Moreover, her ac-
quaintances-become-characters have included prominent literary figures—Edmund Wilson and Philip
Rahv, for example—whose appearances in stories interest critics. Doris Grumbach (*The Company She
Kept*, 1967) explores the real-life sources of Mc-
Carthy's fiction through the publication of *The*

Group in a book that is valuable for critical insights as
well as biographical information. McCarthy is not
reticent about the factual bases of her fiction, but she
confesses to having forgotten in some cases what actually happened and what she made up. A story may be
an accurate report of an event in her life; an autobiographical sketch may draw from imagination to fill
gaps in her memory. We know that the one is story
because the heroine is named Margaret, the other history because she is named Mary.

Even that rather broad clue escaped the notice of
some readers, who took the narrative-essay "Artists in
Uniform" (in *On the Contrary*) for a short story.
McCarthy replies to them in another essay, "Settling
the Colonel's Hash" (also in *On the Contrary*). The
whole point of the "story" was that it really happened,
that it is a "piece of reporting or a fragment of autobiography." Doubtless the mistaken readers allowed
themselves to be misled by the unflattering self-
portrait that the story presents, but such candor is
typical of McCarthy.

In "Artists in Uniform," she tells of an encounter
on a train with an anti-Semitic colonel. Since she does
not volunteer the information, she is dismayed at
being recognized as an artist. The colonel pegs her as a
sculptress, a wrong guess which nevertheless reveals
that her costume, "carefully assembled as it had been
at an expensive shop," was "simply a uniform that
blazed a caste and allegiance just as plainly as the
colonel's khaki and eagles." She likes to regard herself
as something of a missionary in such encounters, appearing as a "normal member of the public" rather
than as an artist or intellectual whose views would
naturally be suspect. In arguing with the colonel about
the Jews, she also withholds the fact that she has a
Jewish grandmother, and she informs him that anti-
Semitism violates God's law, even though she does not

believe in God (neither, somewhat to her surprise, does he). She gets her "comeuppance," however, as they are parting; the colonel asks her married name, and when she says "Broadwater" and begins to spell it for him, she sees a look of comprehension come over his face as he triumphantly misunderstands the name to be Jewish.

Thus, for all her superiority, she has lost the argument with this ignorant, doggedly bigoted man to whom anti-Semitism is, as she has seen, one of his most proudly "intellectual" exercises. The irony of the conclusion turns against her, the well-meaning liberal, the one to whom much is given. "Settling the Colonel's Hash" responds to the readers who treated "Artists in Uniform" as fiction and criticized, on artistic grounds, the choice of hash for the colonel's lunch or sought the meaning of the "symbols"—the shades of green McCarthy was wearing, for example, which were not, she makes clear, somehow references to shades of prejudice but were merely the colors of her attire. She uses the subject as a springboard for a discussion of symbolism and, finally, for an explication of the narrative.

The readers' confusion is perhaps understandable. McCarthy and her fictional characters travel a lot, and this autobiographical piece reads like a story in which another version of Margaret Sargent gets into an argument instead of into bed with an acquaintance on a train. Indeed, two of Margaret's stories are autobiographical, McCarthy said in an interview with Elisabeth Niebuhr, including "The Man in the Brooks Brothers Shirt," which was

an attempt to describe something that really happened— though naturally you have to do a bit of name-changing and city-changing. And the first story, the one about the divorce: that was a stylization—there were no proper

names in it or anything—but still, it was an attempt to be
as exact as possible about something that had happened.[1]

In the same interview, McCarthy went on to describe
her other novels and short stories as "on the whole"
fictional: "What I really do is take real plums and
put them in an imaginary cake. . . . If you're interested
in the cake, you get rather annoyed with people saying what species the real plum was."

The first story in *The Company She Keeps*,
"Cruel and Barbarous Treatment," introduces a young
woman whose name is not given; in the second story
she is identified as Margaret Sargent, but here she is
the Woman With A Secret, a married woman having
an affair, "she." The point of view is grammatically in
the third person, but everything is seen through her
eyes, and she sees herself and two men as acting out
the drama of her life.

She is not critical of the play, but it is pretty bad
stuff, cliché-ridden and depthless. The text capitalizes
the designations of the main characters—the Young
Man, the Husband—and of crucial scenes, providing a
kind of orthographic stage bill. After deciding that it
is "not, in the end, enough to be a Woman With A
Secret if to one's friends one appeared to be a woman
without a secret," the heroine goes on through The
Situation Is Impossible, the Announcement to a few
close friends, and Telling Her Husband. Afterward,
she is terrified lest she has "prolonged the drama beyond its natural limits" and violated artistic propriety,
lest the divorce and remarriage will "constitute an anticlimax." Yet there is nowhere to go but forward. She
plans for her husband to see her off to Reno, but he is
off to what she fears is a "Gay Week-End in the country," and she suffers instead her lover's version of a
farewell scene—riding to 125th Street with her, blow-
ing kisses, running down the platform after the depart-

ing train—which seems to her vulgar and humiliating.

She knows now that she will not marry him, and she is angry with herself as she contemplates the "terror of spinsterhood," which, as a married woman, she had forgotten. But she takes heart from the thought that the Young Divorcee can be glamorous, too, played as a *femme fatale* above "considerations of safety, provisions against loneliness and old age," which are "not only Philistine but irrelevant." When other passengers ask where she is going, she thinks that it will be best "to say 'West' at first, with an air of vagueness and hesitation. Then, when pressed, she might go so so far as to say 'Nevada.' But no farther."

This young woman takes her roles ready-made, choosing the ones that are daring yet fashionable and in good taste and hoping to elicit the slightly shocked admiration of her friends. Investing nothing of herself in the events of her life, she is free to play to whatever she perceives as the expectations of her audience— whether by fulfilling or surprising them—on the basis of aesthetics uncomplicated by emotion. She does not recognize this selflessness as a regrettable defect; her belief that it is "more amusing and more gratifying to play herself than to interpret any character conceived by a dramatist" is sadly ironic.

There is little to know about the company she keeps, restricted as we are to the young woman's view of the other characters. The husband sadly lets her go; the young man seems rather frantic in his devotion. Of the friends whose opinions are so important we see nothing, but references to "two or three" of her closest friends and "these luncheon companions, her dearest friends," suggest more "closest" friends than real ones. They matter so much, however, that the young woman begins to lose interest in the young man when she suspects that they do not share her enthusiasm for him.

She is at last very much alone with a broken marriage and a ruined affair. But what should be a recognition scene is incomplete, for when she recoils from
the vision of her future as a spinster, berates herself
for "burning her bridges," and sees that the young
man simply will not do, she is inspired not to self-
knowledge but to self-justification:

. . . she had possibly been impelled by unconscious forces
to behave more intelligently than appearances would indi-
cate. She was perhaps acting out in a sort of hypnotic
trance a ritual whose meaning had not yet been revealed to
her, a ritual which required, first of all, that the Husband
be eliminated from the cast of characters.

She is prepared to go on with the show.

In "Cruel and Barbarous Treatment" we see Margaret chiefly as she hopes her friends see her. In
"Rogue's Gallery" we hardly see her at all; the subject
is Mr. Sheer, and what we learn of Margaret is what
she reveals incidentally in her account of her dealings
with him and through her voice as first-person nar-
rator—a point of view explained, however feebly, by
an authorial footnote that the piece is an excerpt from
memoirs begun by the heroine.

Mr. Sheer is a "dealer in objects of art," but the
only profitable item at his command is miniature portraits of dogs, painted by an elderly Frenchman and
set into crystal cufflinks. Rich people take advantage
of this unusual means of immortalizing their pets in
numbers sufficient to keep The Savile Galleries smelling of the artist's models all the hot summer that Margaret works as Mr. Sheer's stenographer.

Mr. Sheer—whose name is rich with associations
of elusiveness, transparency, imperiled tenacity—
intensely admires his stock. He loves "any kind of
ingenuity—boxes with false bottoms . . . little statues
that became fountains, Victorian banks made to re-

semble birds' nests." He deplores modern art and is
"puzzled and annoyed . . . that anyone should, for
example, make a set of book ends that looked, simply,
like themselves . . . art was in his eyes a splendid
confidence game." Margaret gradually learns that the
business is founded on nothing; the cherished "possessions" are on consignment, but Mr. Sheer thrives on
dangers which unnerve Margaret. His "business tragedy" is that

> he was continually being forced, by the impatience of a
> creditor, to sell somebody else's property below cost. In
> order to make good in the Bierman case he had had to sell
> an eight-hundred-dollar bronze for six hundred, and to
> make good for the bronze he would have to sell a thousand-
> dollar tapestry for eight hundred.

As the summer wears on, the supply of stationery runs
out, the telephone is disconnected, and the typewriter
is taken away. Margaret, without the means of performing her duties, quits.

She returns from time to time, partly to collect
back pay, but finally Mr. Sheer is gone without leaving a forwarding address. More than a year later, Margaret runs into him. He now specializes in horse sculptures and, fearing immediate ruin, is in "bouyant
spirits." Two days later he calls from jail, but the next
day she can find him neither in jail nor at the fine new
gallery, which is being dismantled. Several years later,
however, Mr. Sheer reappears, having achieved success. He now has his own department of a thriving
business; his specialty is objects relating to sport. His
clientele of rich dog and horse people is a valuable
market, and his associates keep careful watch over
him.

He is not happy in his new status. "It's a funny
thing," he tells Margaret in the course of their renewed friendship, "but you're the only person I have a

good time with any more." Only when Margaret sees
him off to the hospital for a gall bladder operation
does his old "calamitous humor" revive: "It's a very
dangerous operation, Margaret; it may be the death of
me," he tells her. "And for the first time in many
weeks he giggled irrepressibly."

Mr. Sheer is indestructible though sorely be-
sieged. Dishonest, ineducable, impatient of "picayune
distinctions between period replicas and originals by a
master," he recognizes the uselessness of his real talents when he can sell things "on their merits." "In his
eyes, the price being equal, it was better to sell a
Gobelin tapestry as a Beauvais than to sell it as a
Gobelin." He is a fraud, but this is not a defect but
rather an affirmation of character. He needs Margaret
because only she can enjoy with him the contrast between his shady past and his respectable present.

Margaret, too, is a fraud, but in this story her
other life is mentioned only fleetingly: she wonders
how to describe this "dreary job" to her family and
friends, and the fact that the often-unpaid employee
sometimes buys her employer's meals signals another
world to which she belongs, another stage on which
she performs, another Margaret. Here, indeed, she is
not performing. She need not impress Mr. Sheer.
Their first bond was honest economics: she needed a
job, he needed a stenographer, and she took the job
and did her best with it. She is motivated by conscien-
tiousness, good will, amusement, and finally affection.

Although superior to Mr. Sheer, Margaret is his
sympathetic and loyal friend. Unlike him, she can use
long words and see the difference between Byzantine
and baroque, but so much the better; he admires these
abilities and finds them useful. The two of them appreciate each other. Margaret's is the greater awareness, to be sure; she is capable of a self-knowledge and
growth that simply would not interest Mr. Sheer, but

these picayune distinctions are irrelevant to their common good, the ease they find in each other's company. In her account of Mr. Sheer, Margaret is without superciliousness or self-consciousness.

But Mr. Sheer challenges only her ingenuity and tolerance, which she can extend without risk. The friendship, sexless and nonpolitical, even asocial, is private. "The Man in the Brooks Brothers Shirt" is, as Libby of *The Group* would say, another pair of gloves. Margaret is back in character as the young sophisticate, but this time it is an honest and self-critical "she" whose point of view is used. Margaret is on a train again, traveling to Portland to tell Aunt Clara that she is to be married again, though not, or course, to the Young Man of the first story.

In the club car where she first sees the Man, she decides that he looks "like a middle-aged baby, like a young pig, like something in a seed catalogue," "plainly Out of the Question." Nonetheless she and the Man signal to each other from their separate conversations. Although it would be simpler to leave the car than to remain and be picked up—"the whole thing would be so vulgar; one would expose oneself so to the derision of the other passengers"—Margaret settles back to wait, reading an advance copy of an avant-garde novel and expecting the man to be impressed.

But he is not as simple as he looks; he has even read something by the author of the unpublished novel. Margaret accepts his "perfectly proper" invitation to his compartment for a drink. As passersby peer in, she enjoys a double image of herself, supposing that to them she is the great lady in these expensive surroundings, but to Mr. Breen the Bohemian Girl. He evokes a response from her liberal heart when he says that he would like to vote for the Socialist presidential candidate, Norman Thomas. Margaret tries to see him as a frustrated socialist or man of sensibility whom

she can "release from the chains of habit," but he
keeps "clanking those chains comfortably and im-
pudently in her face."

Still, he is no *ordinary* business man. He and the
little adventure have a "human appeal" that she yields
to, "against her judgment." They talk of his liberal
wife, Leonie, and of Margaret's former husband, the
memory of whom now fills her with horror: "How
could I have done it?" she wonders, hurrying on to
talk of her love affairs. Finally she confides in the man
that her favorite quotation is "I am myn owene
woman, wel at ese," although like Chaucer's Criseyde,
she is less her own woman than she hopes.

She wakes the next morning remembering that
she has been drunk, thankful that nothing happened
but discovering that she is naked in bed with a man—
the scene is distinctly reminiscent of the fifteen-year-
old Mary's experience with Bob Berdan. Her horror
grows as memories come back piecemeal; yearningly,
she envisions herself "in a black dress, her face
scrubbed and powdered, her hair neatly combed, sitting standoffishly in her seat." Desperately trying to
realize the image, she scrambles into her clothes, fas-
tening her mended pants with a little brass pin; but
before she can find her garter, the man stirs and pro-
claims his love for her and his intention of divorcing
Leonie. "I was tight," she protests. "A girl like you
doesn't let a man have her just because she's drunk,"
he responds. The exchange ends with Margaret vomit-
ing into the toilet, that "indecent" feature of the
Pullman compartment, thinking "bitterly" that "surely
nothing worse than this could ever happen to her."

Mr. Breen knows how to handle these things.
He has even "squared" the porter, about whom
Margaret inquires, anxious that he who made the bed
may know who slept in it. "He thinks you're wonderful. He said to me, 'Mr. Breen, you sure done better

than most.' " After a moment's feeling that she cannot bear it, Margaret giggles at the vulgarity. If the episode can be seen "in farcical terms," she can "accept, and even, wryly, enjoy it."

They make love again, and then Mr. Breen sends her off to take a bath. Afterward, they share a "ceremonial feast" of breakfast. Margaret knows now that she will not marry her fiancé. In Cleveland, on her return trip, Mr. Breen meets the train. He has sent her "several pieces of glamour-girl underwear and a topaz brooch," and he is bearing a bottle of whiskey and two "garish purple orchids." His interest is already flagging, however, for even while begging Margaret to marry him, he talks of business and of a vacation trip he is planning with Leonie. When he visits in New York, he is critical of her apartment. She knows that his "splurge" is at last over when she receives a letter dictated to his secretary. Always sentimental about her father, he hears, somehow, of her father's death, for he sends a telegram: "SINCEREST CONDOLENCES. YOU HAVE LOST THE BEST FRIEND YOU WILL EVER HAVE."

Mr. Breen is not, as Margaret first thought, sensitive and discriminating; he is appreciative of experience, but what he has is not a sensibility but an appetite. He is merely voracious—at first Margaret sees him as a "young pig," and she sees him grow even more "porcine" in the alcoholic haze of his compartment—and even a little violent in sex. Without taste, he has the prudence to choose name brands: Brooks Brothers clothing and a Vassar wife, the conservatism of the one nicely balanced by the liberalism of the other. He has a human warmth and accessibility, enhanced by a modest intelligence, by humor, and, as Margaret ruefully admits to herself, by money.

Margaret simply flatters herself by thinking that he displays an unusual shrewdness in liking *her*, so unordinary and unconventional. She is attractive, witty, and sympathetic; why shouldn't he like her? Nice himself, assuming that she is nice, the man associates sex and love and in effect expects to make an honest woman of this nice girl whom he has slept with. His mind runs in well-worn tracks. Margaret, he predicts, will come to no good: "In a few years, you'll be one of those Bohemian horrors with oily hair and long earrings." He talks of his pleasure in meeting "different" people. "Golly," he says, "if I were a writer like you!" It is the universal cry of the nonliterate to the literate; the craft of writing is negligible, and wasted to boot on people who don't know any good stories. He believes that Margaret needs a man to look after her; if not he, then her father, who should keep her at home in Portland. The hopelessness of his vulgarity is finally and cruelly demonstrated by his gifts.

In this story, Margaret also is painfully exposed. The brass pin, the rope that holds a suitcase closed, and rundown shoe are tangible evidence that this young woman is less well assembled than she might be. She is vulnerable and beset by self-doubts. Thinking that it is "not really romantic to be the-girl-who-sits-in-the-club-car-and-picks-up-men," she remembers Aunt Clara's warnings against cheapening herself; and she wonders about the book. Since it was actually given to her by a publisher's assistant,

she could not be accused of insincerity. Unless it could be that her whole way of life had been assumed for purposes of ostentation. . . . If it had not been this book, it would have been something else, which would have served equally well to impress a pink middle-aged stranger.

She is the one who is impressed, however, by Mr. Breen's command of things. His "connoisseurship" pleases her and prompts her to conclude that the men

previously attracted to her have been in some way
"disqualified" and therefore "humble in love," including her reliable but "peculiar-looking" former
husband and her handsome but good-for-nothing fiancé. Despite her high-minded contempt for the
business world, she sees Mr. Breen as coming from the
"center of things where choice is unlimited" and exults
that he has "chosen *her*."

Words like "ritualistic," "ceremonial," and even
"farcical" signal that Margaret is still performing, still
referring action to patterns by which it can be judged
aesthetically. She is pleased with her role until she decides that Mr. Breen is too old for her and that once
again she has taken a "lame duck" lover: "If she had
met him ten years before, would he have chosen her
then?" While bathing, she reorganizes the little adventure into an allegory in which she reclaims her
wavering superiority and rejoices even in the brass
pin. Ineffectual as it has been in its literal function, it
still symbolizes poverty and the "citadel of socialist
virginity" which can be taken by the rich businessman
but "never truly subdued."

The man's whole assault on her . . . was an incidental atrocity in the long class war. She smiled again, thinking that
she had come out of it untouched, while he had been reduced to jelly.

Far from it. Mr. Breen will fade painlessly from Margaret's life. He is untouched; but she, if not precisely
reduced to a jelly, will continue a diminished journey.
Literally, she has no news for Aunt Clara, and the trip
to Portland is pointless.

Reluctantly returning to the compartment after
the bath, Margaret knows that she must see "this absurd, ugly love story to a conclusion," for that is what
it is and no amount of artistic distancing can free her
from responsibility in it. Her feelings are the problem.

"How," she wondered earlier, "can you act upon feelings if you don't know what they are?" But she had a fundamental distaste for Mr. Breen from the moment she first saw him. Instead of acting upon that feeling, she played her role, drank too much, and engaged *his* feelings. In the aftermath, she had a shattering insight: "*Dear Jesus, . . . I'm really as hard as nails.*" The second act of love was an effort at atonement. "*This,*" she thought, "*is going to be the only real act of charity I have ever performed in my life; it will be the only time I have ever given anything when it honestly hurt me to do so.*"

Now, she makes the man the gift of a perfect adventure. "Right now, I think I can live on this one day for the rest of my life," he tells her. She quietly lets him slip away, in his own way and time, without spoiling it for him. There is no anguish, no breakup. After his last visit, Margaret is alone "trying to decide whether to eat in a tearoom or cook herself a chop," and we recall that "women alone look conspicuous and forlorn in good restaurants"; tearooms are part of the terror of spinsterhood anticipated by the young woman of "Cruel and Barbarous Treatment." Now, however, the thought is not foremost in Margaret's mind. She feels "flat and sad" but glad that she never told Mr. Breen of the broken engagement. In sparing Bob Breen, she has performed an act of love and expiation; she has begun to question the role she plays in the company she keeps.

Margaret is often alone. She makes two solitary journeys, she divorces her husband, and she breaks two engagements. She is alone at a gallery, and again at a theater, when she runs into Mr. Sheer. She is alone after her last meeting with Mr. Breen; later, when she tears up his telegram because "it would have been dreadful if anyone had seen it," we have no idea who "anyone" could be.

In "The Genial Host," Margaret goes to a party. Pflaumen, the host, is a dull man brilliantly portrayed, right down to the carefully assembled art objects which adorn his apartment and await the notice of his guests. The guests, too, are carefully assembled, being variously "interesting" or successful. Margaret is interesting. The story is told in the second person, the "affectionate, diminutive 'you,' " a rare and in this case peculiarly effective narrative device. The heroine has been "she" and "I"; now she is "you," and the reader is drawn willy-nilly into the character:

He held out his arms to help you with your coat. . . . If you did not know him well, you did not realize that he loved you for that patched fur. It signified that you were the *real thing*, the poet in a garret. . . .

At the same time that "you" are Margaret, individual and unique, you are also one of a succession of actors cast in the part, useful to Pflaumen, being briefed by an old hand: this is the way it goes.

In Pflaumen's artificial world, personality becomes "unequivocal and defiant": "If you asserted your Trotskyism, your poverty, your sexual freedom, the expectant mother radiated her pregnancy, the banker basked in his reactionary convictions. . . . Everybody, for the moment, knew exactly who he was." You terrify and delight yourself with a rude and politically unfashionable outburst, and when Pflaumen "tenderly" explains that "Meg is a violent Trotskyist," you are ashamed because you are just showing off. But you have made an impression: the publisher has some work for you, the Berolzheimers want you to come to dinner, and Erdman, the Marxist, will, you think, become your lover. Riding high, you snub Pflaumen's tentative question about you and Erdman; you send him to get you a highball, but he turns to ask, "in a true stage whisper," "You're not drinking too much,

are you?" Pflaumen, who lives vicariously, wants
"part of your life" in exchange for the benefits you
have reaped from the association with him, and he will
punish disloyalty. Still, you feel superior, but as you
prepare to leave, he strikes again. Inviting Erdman to
come again, he adds pointedly, "And bring your wife.
. . . You ought to meet her, Meg." You leave alone,
knowing that you must break with Pflaumen, but "not
yet, not while you were still so poor, so loverless, so
lonely."

Margaret's friendship with Pflaumen is unpleasantly symbiotic. "Bought" by his "wines and rich
food and prominent acquaintances," wearing her
shabby fur, she comes, at Pflaumen's direction, to act
her part in the little morality play. Pflaumen's pleasure
in her outburst justifies a suspicion that with her out-
spokenness and wit, and her tendency to drink too
much, Meg fairly often provides moments of heightened drama, and that this habit enhances her value to
her genial host. This is Pflaumen's play, not Margaret's.

Her other friends are glimpsed in contrast to
Pflaumen, whose invitations are so ceremoniously issued. They call up "to demand, 'Are you free Thurs-
day?' before disclosing whether they [want her] to
picket a movie house, attend a lecture at the New
School, buy tickets for a party for Spain, or go and
dance at a new night club." They sound terribly active—"pink," of course, as Mr. Breen would say, but
the liberal intellectuals' revulsion against Communism
came only toward the end of the decade, as the blood-
iness of the Stalin regime in Russia became apparent
and Margaret's efforts on behalf of Trotsky were vindicated. What troubles her about her political opinions
is not that they may be wrong but that she may hold
them for wrong reasons.

The theme of politics, prominent in the two pre-
ceding stories, is central in "Portrait of the Intellectual

as a Yale Man"; again, for Margaret, politics and sex
are hopelessly entangled. The outburst at Pflaumen's
party was an attempt to attract the attention of, and
claim kinship with, the Marxist Erdman. In "Portrait,"
political liberalism is one basis of a brief affair. The
point of view, indeed, the story, is Jim Barnett's; we
see Margaret only as he does. She is introduced to him
as "our gay divorcee" when she is hired by the *Liberal*, the magazine for which Jim writes. As her tea
grows cold, she speaks in a "breathless voice" to a
fascinated audience, telling anecdotes about Reno and
defending Trotsky. It is our first view of her from
outside.

"A troublemaker," Jim judges her to his wife.
"Too tense," he thinks, as if she "lived on excitement,
situations, crises, trouble," speaking up though "scared
stiff." He sees her lingering at a subway entrance like a
girl without a date or appearing as "the extra girl" at a
political dinner (the terrors of spinsterhood again).
Her honesty and intensity remind him unpleasantly of
his calm and compromised life, of his proper, practical
wife and his proper, practical politics.

Jim Barnett has, however, discovered socialism,
and he writes about it. Whereas "most men had come
to socialism by some all-too-human compulsion—they
were out of work or lonely or sexually unsatisfied,"
Jim "came to socialism freely, from the happy center
of things." His presence on the left lent it respectabil-
ity, for "nobody could possibly object to socialism if
it were going to run by earnest, undogmatic Yale
men." Jim learned at Yale not to admire anything too
"whole-heartedly," but to keep himself "accessible,
undecided."

He is therefore wary of Meg, and he concludes
that there must be something wrong with her. But
two months later he kisses her in a taxi on the way to a
political dinner, and the next night he goes to bed with

her. The affair is completed in two meetings. His "lust" demands satisfaction and achieves it "with a zeal . . . somehow both businesslike and insane." Afterward he avoids her.

But when Meg announces her support of the Socialist-Labor presidential candidate, Jim, out of a "sense of chivalry," announces for the Socialist, Norman Thomas. He cannot be so "outlandish" as Margaret, but he can descend from the "far too comfortable" Roosevelt bandwagon and make a bridge between her and the rest of the staff. He signs a statement demanding a hearing and the right of asylum for Trotsky because of the "purely sporting question involved—you don't accuse a man without giving him a chance to answer for himself." To his discomfort, however, Margaret is again being "intense."

When he realizes at last that the *Liberal* has "effectively purged itself of Trotskyism" without taking a public stand, Jim is in a shameful position. He needs a way to "demonstrate his political seriousness without embroiling himself," and Margaret's dismissal provides him with a way. He resigns from his job in protest, a gesture neither political nor chivalrous, and plans to write an important Marxist book. But he goes to work for an illustrated popular magazine with a conservative point of view; well paid and successful, he takes pride in never having time for "his own" work, and he enjoys both success and the sympathy of his friends, who regard his career as a "tragedy of waste" inflicted on him by his wife's incessant material demands. Margaret's role has been that of the spoiler, the wrecker: she taught him the "cage of his own nature" by speaking more truth than he cared to hear.

Margaret's impact on Jim is ironic, for we know how she distrusts her motives, how she suspects herself of using politics as a way of getting attention and asserting her superiority; if it is fashionable for liberals

to admire Stalin, she cannot be sure that her support
of Trotsky is not merely a way going them one better.
But looking at her through Jim Barnett's eyes, we see
nothing of this. Where their paths have crossed, he has
had little awareness of her but uncomfortable awareness of himself.

From the great distance of Jim's point of view,
the final episode moves abruptly to the intimacy of the
analyst's couch. In "Ghostly Father, I Confess," Margaret is again a wife desiring a divorce, as she was at the
beginning. The point of view is Margaret's, and the
story is an account of a session with Dr. James; its
substance is partly their conversation, partly Margaret's thoughts. All of her fragmented selves respond
to Dr. James. Margaret the role player wants to impress him and keeps trying to catch in his eyes "an
expression of disapproval, of astonishment or regret—
anything but that kindly neutrality." Margaret the
snob analyzes her analyst and finds him wanting: "She
would spend half a session trying to show him, say,
that a man they both knew was a ridiculous character,
that a movie they had both seen was cheap. And it
would be hopeless, absolutely hopeless, for he *was* that
man, he *was* that movie." Margaret the *femme fatale*
preens herself because he compliments her: "*He likes
me*," she thinks; "*he likes me the best*." But Margaret
the self-doubter rejects his compliments as a "thera-
peutic lie."

Her husband, Frederick, an architect, has "done
what the modern, liberal man inevitably does—called
in an expert" to deal with his difficult wife. Margaret
wants to leave him, but the tyrannical and overbearing
Frederick will not allow it. He accuses her of using
her "wonderful scruples" as an excuse for "acting like
a bitch." Dr. James murmurs about "early religious
training" and "moral standards that nobody could live
up to." Margaret feels that her most valued attributes

—her sense of truth and her scruples—are slipping away under a double attack.

Margaret and Dr. James look to her childhood for explanations of her unhappiness. In deference to her dead mother's Catholicism, her father had entrusted her upbringing to her mother's sister, Aunt Clara, who created in his house a grim, ascetic, joyless life for his daughter; thus Margaret was the "Catholic child of a Protestant father, the shabby daughter of a prosperous lawyer, the underbred Irish offspring of a genteel New England parent." Eventually the aunt was overthrown—Margaret lost her faith—and a new girl emerged, pretty, well dressed, and remarkable only for an "air of coming from nowhere." After years of marveling over her escape, Margaret found during her first marriage that she was not free at all, that in her furious outbursts against her husband she was "exactly like Aunt Clara." Now in her second marriage she is, Dr. James tells her, reenacting her childhood. Frederick, who is older than Margaret, is both the tyrannical Aunt Clara and the apparently indifferent father.

Leaving Dr. James's office, Margaret remembers a dream she never finished telling him. She was in a cabin on an outing, part of her orientation at Eggshell College, along with some "low-class" girls and three young men of "a sort of dun color, awkward, heavy-featured, without charm, a little like the pictures of Nazi prisoners. . . ." She flirts with one, and his appearance is transformed. He kisses her, but when she looks up, she sees that he is once again like the others. Again, his face refines, but when he kisses her this time she keeps her eyes closed, "knowing very well what she would see if she opened them."

It was only a dream. Yet she cannot "disown" the dream or its self-accusation:

It was she who was the Nazi prisoner, the pseudo-Byron, the equivocal personality who was not truly protean but only appeared so. And yet, she thought, walking on, she could still detect her own frauds. At the end of the dream, her eyes were closed, but the inner eye remained alert.

The story ends with a prayer—"If the flesh must be blind, let the spirit see. Preserve me in disunity"—and the admission that she cannot be "too demanding, for unfortunately, she did not believe in God."

A former Catholic, Margaret frequently thinks in religious terms. With Mr. Breen, she was pleased by the paradox that her act of sacrifice required mortification of the flesh through the act of pleasure, and she startlingly imagined her naked body as a "slab of white lamb on an altar." Ashamed of her Trotskyist outburst at Pflaumen's party, she judges her own a greater blasphemy than Peter's: "social pressure . . . made Peter deny the Master," but made her affirm him. It was "the difference between plain and fancy cowardice." Her Catholic unbringing has provided a metaphoric language, but she has no faith, and the "ghostly father" to whom she confesses is just the pragmatic Dr. James.

Margaret is nonetheless answerable to truth and to her scruples, which deprive her of comfort she might take in right action. Politically, she supports the cause of the downtrodden, but she judges herself harshly for it.

The truth was that . . . her proletarian sympathies constituted a sort of snub that she administered to the middle class, just as a really smart woman will outdress her friends by relentlessly underdressing them. Scratch a socialist and you find a snob.

Snob though she is, Margaret lacks discrimination; aloof and superior, she is yet susceptible to the most unsuitable men. Dr. James is another version of Mr. Breen, through whom Margaret hoped to learn something about herself. Ending the session positively, he encourages Margaret to free herself with her mind, adding, "That and your beauty are the two weapons you have." Self-consciously preparing to leave, Margaret thinks, "my beauty," and "Well, well!" On the street she sees her folly: even if Dr. James does "like" her "the best," he is still a "fussy, methodical young man whom she would never ordinarily have looked at."

Yet what she "ordinarily" does has yielded a "divorce, three broken engagements, a whole series of love affairs abandoned *in medias res*," and a second unhappy marriage. Margaret habitually and unselectively seeks masculine attention, but when she enjoys a little victory over the conventional Aunt Clara, it is on Aunt Clara's terms. Recalling her words—"It doesn't pay to let men think you're easy"—Margaret smiles to herself "patronizingly" because she is going to tell Aunt Clara that she is getting married again. In her horror of spinsterhood, her flirtation with Erdman, her "affairs" with Jim Barnett and Mr. Breen, Margaret reveals the depth of self-doubt that is inadequately disguised by her superior and unconventional manner, but she reveals it even more clearly in her attitude toward getting married. She wants to be—and is equipped to be—her own woman, "wel at ese," but she keeps yearning toward that conventional happy ending for the conventional woman.

In a "Foreword" to the novel, McCarthy compares the progress of the novel to a search. Finding the "ordinary, indispensable self" missing from her "spiritual pocketbook," the heroine, accompanied by the reader, retraces her steps looking for it. "It is not only scenes and persons but points of view that are revisited—the intimate 'she,' the affectionate diminutive 'you,' the thin, abstract, autobiographical 'I.' "

Margaret and Dr. James practice conventional psychology in seeking the lost identity in the agonized

childhood, when one personality followed another
without developing from it, but to locate a source is
not to solve a problem; and Dr. James's advice to
Margaret to win her freedom now as she did then is
facile and pointless. He thinks that if she "wins" her
freedom from Frederick, she will not want to use it.
This would, to be sure, solve her husband's problem,
but freedom, used or unused, will not supply the missing self. The episodes of Margaret's life do not cohere
any more than they did in childhood. Mr. Sheer's
friend hardly resembles Jim Barnett's "intense" lover,
and neither of them is much like the shallow role
player of "Cruel and Barbarous Treatment."

"Preserve me in disunity," Margaret prays, having understood the dream that she never told Dr.
James. Her susceptibility to "love" reflects a failure of
self-love; she looks to others for an image of herself to
love, and in doing so she plays different selves for all
the company she keeps. That is why the attentions of
Mr. Breen or the praise of Dr. James are at once important and dangerous. That is why she requires an
audience. Now, at last, she can see the painful but
valuable truth that she avoided at the end of "Cruel
and Barbarous Treatment."

In calling *The Company She Keeps* a novel, we
are using McCarthy's designation of the book, but we
are using the term very loosely. Each of the six episodes
is self-contained; taken together, however, they are
phases of Margaret's quest for self—a single heroine
and a single action. But there is little interweaving of
materials. In "The Man in the Brooks Brothers Shirt,"
Margaret is "suffused with horror" to recall her treatment of her husband; "Portrait of the Intellectual as a
Yale Man" refers to a trip west and a broken engagement; "Ghostly Father, I Confess" mentions the man
on the train. But there is not much such cross-refer-
encing, and what there is does not convince. Perhaps it

is appropriate that the stories are inadequately bound together by the elusive character of the heroine, since the point is the disunity of her personality, still, the book reads like short stories; and to discern a novel running through them requires an effort. They are, however, excellent short stories, especially "Cruel and Barbarous Treatment" and "The Man in the Brooks Brothers Shirt," at once original, complex, and deftly built.

The kind of heroine that McCarthy uses again and again, created after her own image, is individualized for her diverse roles. Sometimes her biography contains parallels to McCarthy's own, but not again to the degree that Margaret's does. Martha Sinnott of *A Charmed Life*, Kay Petersen of *The Group*, and Rosamund Brown of *Birds of America* all have some personal history in common with McCarthy. Domna Rejnev of *The Groves of Academe* and Sophie Weil of *Cannibals and Missionaries* share her moral and intellectual intensity.

The McCarthy heroine has the advantages of freedom from poverty, of intelligence and a good education, and of physical attractiveness. She has literary or other artistic abilities. She is articulate and outspoken, sophisticated but often extremely self-conscious and given to self-doubt. She has exacting but unconventional standards of conduct which she applies most rigidly but not always successfully to herself. Suspicious of the obvious or the easy, she loves truth and tries never to deceive herself.

In "Characters in Fiction" (*On the Contrary*), McCarthy distinguishes heroes and heroines from comic characters by their ability to learn. We are all heroines or heroes in life, only occasionally glimpsing the comic in ourselves, and we identify with the heroines in fiction, following them "with all our hopes, i.e., with our subjective conviction of human freedom"

—"we put ourselves in their place." Since they can learn, they are capable of change and growth, a capacity denied to comic characters.

"The comic element is the incorrigible element in every human being." But the comic character is not therefore simpler than the hero or heroine; he is "likely to be more complicated and enigmatic . . . fuller of surprises and turnabouts; Mr. Micawber, for instance, can find the most unexpected ways of being himself. . . . It is a sort of resourcefulness." Comic characters are immortal; in their "implacable resistance to change, they are what perdures or remains."

Mr. Breen is such a character; a businessman, a nice guy, complete, he is what he is and will always be. His very name is redolent of commercialism, like a brand name, alliterating with Brooks Brothers but rhyming with *sheen* and *-ine* and suggesting a made-up name for hair dressing. Mr. Sheer, the complete confidence man, is one of several frauds that McCarthy treats with affection, including the vicomte of *A Charmed Life* and the incomparable Mr. Sciarappa, the cicerone in *Cast a Cold Eye.*

A self-appointed guide, Mr. Sciarappa attends a nameless young couple (the young woman is much like Margaret Sargent) through Italy until "he is following us, but he is ahead," the young man concludes, "abandoning historical explanations forever." Mr. Sciarappa is mysterious; he does not like the young couple, and they are fascinated, mystified, bored, and bound to him all at once. Is he a fortune hunter, mistaking them for rich Americans? They refer him to the rich Miss Grabbe (herself a splendid character who regards European men as "a continental commodity" to be enjoyed like any other), but her distressingly candid account of their sexual coupling reveals more of the physical and less of the "more sociological, more humane" side of Mr. Sciarappa

than they want. As guide, he is useless, apparently
unknown to the headwaiters he claims familiarity with
and not drawn to good restaurants in any case. His
finances relate vaguely to silk, but he "did not precisely own a factory, nor was he precisely in the
exporting business." The young couple finally embarrass themselves by looking up his address in Rome,
finding a seedy house in a shabby quarter which tells
them nothing they want to know either about Mr.
Sciarappa or about themselves.

One hesitates to mention Francis (or Frances)
Cleary, "The Friend of the Family" (also in *Cast a
Cold Eye*). This essay or sketch is "really" about the
struggles in marriage, or about compromise, or about
equality. The political implications near the end are
hard to ignore. But certainly the main *substance* of
"The Friend of the Family" is the character of Francis
Cleary, who also comes as a female or as a couple. He
is the neutral friend who can always be substituted for
real friends, over whom the married couple can never
agree. He can be absolutely depended upon never to
be a real friend and therefore the cause of strife; he is
dull but so serviceable that finally versions of Francis
Cleary are all the couple has. As he grows unpleasant
and tyrannical from his centrality in their lives, they
may find that their only escape is to *become* "the
Clearys, say, of Round Hill Road." Louis Auchincloss
considers the "analysis of Cleary as a dope, as an irri-
tant, and as an ultimate menace" to be "perhaps the
most brilliant piece of writing in all of Miss Mc-
Carthy's work."[2]

There are fewer heroines in McCarthy's fiction
than comic characters, and even fewer heroes. Until
her last two novels (*Birds of America* and *Cannibals
and Missionaries*), McCarthy had not created a fully
developed sympathetic male character, with the possible exception of President Hoar in *The Groves of*

Academe. Her men tended to be comic or villainous or, like Bentkoop (*Groves*), mere names assigned to essential arguments. The world according to Mary McCarthy is not corrigible, nor are many of its inhabitants, but that circumstance does not excuse her heroes and heroines from responsibility for right action. Irvin Stock considers a major theme of her fiction to be "how hard it has been for intellectuals in our time to behave decently and humanely" and adds that "there is no safety in good intentions when their pursuit requires us to ignore the truth."[3] Assuming the validity of reason and judgment based on honest observation of facts, McCarthy is consistently a rationalist and a moralist.

4

The Demands of the Ethical
and the Quest for Superiority
in *A Charmed Life*

The McCarthy heroine never leads an unexamined life. To be human is to live deliberately, to control one's affairs. That is why Martha and John Sinnott finally decide to buy the house in New Leeds. They would be returning to the village on the coast of Maine where, seven years earlier, Martha had fled to John and ended her disastrous marriage to Miles Murphy. What made the return to New Leeds seem particularly daring was the fact that Miles lived not far away with his new wife and baby. But Martha was writing a play, and New Leeds, beautiful and remote, seemed a perfect place to work; the Sinnotts had an opportunity to buy a house that she had always admired, and they were "afraid of being afraid to buy it."

The Sinnotts are different from New Leedsians, however. New Leedsians live chaotic, unproductive lives. They drink too much; they are forever in danger, forever getting hurt. But as Martha explains, "Nobody dies. Hardly ever. That's it; they just get crippled." Recognizing potential pitfalls, Martha and John make a point of living well-ordered, ceremonious lives. They work; they dress well; they have "just one cocktail" every day at six except when they embarrass themselves by having just one more.

Although disappointed that they do not have a

child, Martha expects that they soon will have one. Now in their early thirties, she and John are an attractive, romantic couple, and all should be well with them. But the opening chapter reveals the vulnerability of their entire edifice, the house with the small damages wrought by the summer tenant, the marriage with weak spots susceptible to small accidents. John cuts his hand and is annoyed that Martha is, as usual, unsympathetic and clumsy in nursing an injury. When good humor is restored, they have their cocktail and a little more. Slicing an onion to cook with the chicken, Martha cuts her finger. Laughing ruefully, they recognize the sign that they may be like other New Leedsians after all. Martha takes her accident as a warning to have John's more serious cut attended to, and they go to the doctor.

New Leeds has a varied if small population. Martha and John belong to the artistic set, but they are sparing with the time they spend socializing. They are friends of the Coes, who moved to New Leeds ten years before, during the war. Warren Coe is an unknown artist. At fifty, he has sold his canvases only to his father-in-law, but he is undaunted and earnest as he goes on working out theories of time and space, talking about but more avidly listening to "philosophy" which somehow relates to his painting. He was once stricken ill by the realization that time is not visible, but after nearly three weeks in bed he was cured by "Relativity." Much of the action of the novel revolves around one of his pictures, a huge portrait of Martha in a state of fission.

His wife, Jane, "a big, tawny, ruminative girl, now thirty-eight," enjoys the Coes' position as social center of the artistic set. Although wealthy, the Coes live plainly in a modern windswept house on a bluff, more ruined than merely weathered. They serve drinks in jelly glasses, with ice if the refrigerator is

working and soda if Jane remembers to buy it. Warren has not had an ironed shirt for three years, but he
is satisfied with the state of his wardrobe, only occasionally wondering what he will wear to his mother's
funeral when the time comes. Jane has given away his
good clothes, and according to his sister down in Savannah, his mother is very frail.

Martha is a favorite of Warren's; he values her
intelligence and her honesty. Martha is fond of Warren but impatient with his naive "philosophical" questions (she is a former student of philosophy). The
Coes have remained friends with Martha's former
husband, too, and Martha knows this, but even so,
Warren is anxious about entertaining the Murphys
when the annual dinner invitation is issued. But Warren loves to thrill to the brilliance of Miles's mind, and
Jane is curious to know—as the whole community
is—"how Miles Murphy was taking his second wife's
return." Miles is doing very well with Helen, his third,
who is wealthy and "all woman, and he was damn
lucky to have got her," he knows. He remembers
Martha with affection nonetheless, especially when he
has been drinking. Miles "always had a weakness for
intelligent women, though he knew them to be bad
for him." Older than Martha, he has been a "successful
playwright . . . a boxer, practically professional . . . a
psychologist, a lay analyst, a writer of adventure stories, a practicing mystic, a magazine editor."

The Murphys' evening with the Coes complicates
the plot. "Nonplussed" by Warren's portrait of Martha, Miles wants to buy it, and Helen, the perfect wife,
has no objection to his owning a portrait of her prede-
cessor; but the decision, Warren says, must be Martha's. By a not-unlikely coincidence, an unsuspecting
Martha drops in that very evening, she and John
bringing their friend Dolly Lamb to meet the Coes.
Martha is nervous and apprehensive, yet it is clear

what she and Miles had in common: they talk well together. Martha makes no objection to the sale of the painting.

New Leeds boasts among its permanent residents a vicomte with a "rich air of fraudulence" who sells antiques to the summer people and falls back on liquor and wine to tide him through the winter. When he visits Martha and John to purchase a Seth Thomas clock and other objects which came with their house, he refuses a drink—"Dear lady," he protests, "I am an alcoholic"—but later he drinks port at the Coes'. He is equipped with a repertoire of stories which may or may not be true; with a commitment to Catholicism, but also, when there is need, with the name of an abortionist who can help girls in trouble; and with a decidedly practical view of life. He brings the Sinnotts news that the painting has been delivered to Miles and that Warren has charged the extravagant price of $1,800 for it. Martha is indignant. "The truth is that Warren's work is absurd, in the world's eyes. And I expect him to take that into account, when he sets a price on it." The vicomte, more pragmatic, suggests that price is value and that the value of the painting has been set by its sale.

Miles's purchase of her portrait is a disturbing reentry into Martha's life of the man whom she thought she had escaped. She takes Dolly Lamb into her confidence. She explains to Dolly that her marriage to Miles—preceded by her going to bed with him twice when drunk—engendered a continuing "war of principle" between two people who claim to "have the 'lowdown' " on each other and that she will lose because it occurs to her that she may be wrong. "Miles never has that experience." After hearing Martha's confessions—that she is envious of Miles's marriage, that she fears that she wants a baby chiefly in order to have a "better one" than his, that an abortion

"years ago" may prevent her conceiving, that she
came back to New Leeds to show other people how
"tawdry" they are in comparsion to her and John,
even though she hates this in herself—Dolly is left to
tell herself, in "stern bell tones," "You must not be
shocked."

Dolly is past thirty and growing weary of her
own "promise" as an artist, which her meticulous little
paintings fail to fulfill. Martha and John are chiefly
responsible for her coming to New Leeds, and they
assume responsibility for directing her activities there.
Martha has warned Dolly to avoid Sandy Gray as a
time waster. "His fourth wife had just left him. . . .
He would want to be neighborly and advise her about
her painting, but he was only after liquor and somebody to cook his meals for him." When Sandy first
comes "swashing through the pond" and into her little
house, the virginal Dolly is shocked by his presumptu-
ousness; but she decides that he is "gentle," and despite
Martha's warning, she sinks into an unfruitful friendship with him.

The climax of the novel is a reading, in French, of
Racine's tragedy, *Bérénice*, at the Coes' house. The
Coes invite the Murphys, the Sinnotts, the vicomte,
Dolly, and a nondescript retired couple, the Hubers.
Jane has a busy day preparing for the party. Making
her rounds, she finds in the mailbox at the post office a
telegram announcing the death of Warren's mother,
and at a most inconvenient time. There is a storm, and
Warren will not be able to get a plane to Savannah
until it is over in a day or even two. Moreover, the
only suit he might conceivably wear to the funeral is
out of town on the body of its owner, John, and there
is no time to buy a new one and have it fitted. Warren
can, as a matter of fact, do nothing about the death of
his mother before tomorrow. Therefore, Jane reasons,

there is no good reason to tell him about it and spoil the party.

It takes all of Jane's persuasion to get Martha to come without John. By coincidence, Miles shows up alone because the baby is sick and Helen has stayed with it. But the reading proceeds satisfactorily, even with the abbreviated guest list. Afterward, the conversation turns on subjects such as renunciation and sacrifice that were introduced in the play. Warren, romantic and literal, cannot admire Titus's tragic renunciation because he was "engaged to *Bérénice*, darn it," and "he broke his promise to her, just for reasons of state. I call that pretty cheap." Martha and Miles discuss *Hamlet*, in which, Miles explains, "a hero questions . . . the whole apparatus of cognition. He sees differently from the 'normal' people in the play. . . . Is his vision distorted?" A reference to Raskolnikov moves Warren to worry the question of relative values: "I don't want to murder old women, but some other fellow might be made differently. It seems to me you've got to consider that. You've got to give *that* fellow a reason." Miles's reply is incomparable: "For you, it's an academic question. If you don't want to murder old women, let it go at that. Don't worry about the other fellow. Live selfishly."

Eventually Miles takes Martha home, after both have drunk too much. Martha at first resists his advances, but, as he crudely reflects, she is really "too ironic a girl not to see that one screw, more or less, could not make much difference, when she had already laid it on the line for him about five hundred times." It does, however, make a good deal of difference. It frees Martha from the power that Miles has had over her. But the next morning, when John still has not come home, Martha is terrified that he might have come home early and seen her and Miles through the thin curtains. Perhaps he has left her, or perhaps there has been an accident. Only when he arrives safely home is Martha's life restored.

Dolly, meanwhile, has become involved in the affairs of Sandy Gray. He is trying to get custody of his children from his former wife, Clover, and Dolly is a character witness on his behalf. In spite of her eloquent testimony, she is relieved when the judge decides in Clover's favor. Sandy, however, is stricken. That night gives substantiation to a rumor that he is impotent.

Martha, one morning in November, wakes up in the joyful realization that she must be pregnant. She begins planning small economies. She faces the truth that she is already seizing on the pregnancy as an excuse not to finish her play, and she firmly decides to finish it. But in the midst of her joy, she has a terrible thought: The baby could be Miles's. The possibility, though remote, is real, and she might never know the truth. She will have an abortion, but she will have to borrow money for it.

Martha knows that her "apparatus of cognition" is different from other people's. Most people, in New Leeds at least, would agree with the doctor who confirmed the pregnancy and urged her to take comfort in the statistical probability that the baby is John's and the fact that if it is not, no one need ever know. But Warren Coe, to her surprise, understands completely when she goes to him to ask for money. Less complicated than Martha but no less earnest in his love of truth, Warren sees instantly that Martha cannot posit a life—hers or a baby's—on a possible lie.

Warren cannot get money from his own resources without Jane's knowledge, and this secret must be kept from her as from John; but Miles owes, still, for the portrait, and Warren enjoys the irony of collecting from Miles to lend to Martha. The scene in which he tries to do so provides the now fiery little artist with unwelcome truth about Miles, who not only refuses him the money but personally and artistically insults him and bellows to his wife to get the "bill-collector" out of his study. Warren finally gets the money from his mother's estate, as an advance, and there remains only for Martha to get it from him. When he calls, inviting the Sinnotts to tea, Martha and John quarrel over the invitation, and Martha starts off alone, later returning to tell John that she loves him before leaving again. John was almost ready to leave her, but now the meaning of her recent erratic behavior dawns on him. She has been scheming to buy him an expensive Christmas present; it is so characteristic of her.

An "exalted" Martha leaves the Coes' house after declining an invitation to stay for cocktails with "local poetess" Eleanor Considine, who is expected at any moment. Martha hums as she drives. Once it is all over, she may tell John and have "truth between them" again, but she wonders whether the impulse is pointless sentimentality. She knows, at least, that whatever she decides, it will be "all right." She is no longer afraid of herself. But now, seeing headlights reflected from around a blind curve ahead, she concentrates on driving and hugs her side of the road. The other driver would be Eleanor Considine, on her way to the Coes'. As the cars collide head-on, Martha thinks, "in a wild flash of humor," that she has made a "fatal mistake: in New Leeds, after sundown, she would have been safer on the wrong side of the road."

The major flaw of the novel is apparent even in summary. Eleanor Considine, a woman of letters who insists on considering herself Martha's rival, is unceremoniously invented a scant three pages from the end, characterized as a "cautionary example of everything Martha was trying not to be," and put into an

automobile which, naturally, she drives on the wrong
side of the road. She has not been mentioned before,
yet here she is, complete with a brief biography to
demonstrate the irony of the fatal meeting. She once
ran away from a "conventional husband"; her young
second husband "died of tetanus, all alone, in Mexico,
from a cut she had neglected to have attended to." A
"scribbler" of fifty, she is known for her "artless, witty
candor." She has dyed red hair and a "rough, ringing
laugh."

Martha has something in common with this
woman; but Martha had her husband's cut attended to,
she is not artless, she does not dye her hair or have a
rough laugh, and she does not drive on the wrong side
of the road. She is made of finer stuff. That is the point
of her story, which McCarthy calls a kind of fairy
tale. Martha's name—*sin not*—is descriptive more of
aspiration than of achievement, but her return to New
Leeds is a test of her superiority not merely to the rest
of the residents but to her own past. The village has
preserved seven-year-old gossip which would suggest
that she was quite in her milieu—of Martha leaving
her husband's house in a transparent nightgown, steal-
ing his Plymouth, deserting her child, joining her
lover. There is just enough distorted half-truth in the
story to trouble her.

Born in far-away Alaska, daughter of a Swedish
engineer and an Italian music teacher, Martha Sinnott
could be a fairy-tale heroine. "A strange, poetical-
looking being, with very fair, straight hair drawn in a
little knot, a quaint oval face, very dark, wide-set eyes,
and a small, slight figure," she has been an actress, a
translator, and a student of philosophy; she loves
domesticity and is living happily ever after with the
prince who rescued her. In the first chapter, she is
sewing curtains, wearing a gold thimble. "Like the
wife sewing in the fairy tale, Martha was wishing for a

child." Later, she reflects sadly that the New Leeds experience has been like "a fairy tale, in which you get your wish, but in such a way that you wished you had not wished it."

The magic period of seven years has passed since she and John met—the fatal time span for a marriage, they once agreed. But she is in a neverland, out of time and place. New Leeds has minimal commerce with the outside world. There is a summer influx of tourists and part-time residents, but that season has passed and there remain the feckless natives. They appear in the form of a largely pregnant girl—unmarried, of course —waiting in the doctor's anteroom when Martha emerges from his office; and they dress up in their best "conventional" clothes to come to court as character witnesses for Sandy or Clover, presenting a most peculiar pageant to Dolly's bewildered view. But they are remote from Martha's society, which is composed of artists and intellectuals, has-beens and would-bes in a state of retirement or escape from even the minimal reality of New Leeds itself. They are rich, like the Coes, or poor with "tiny" incomes, like the Sinnotts. They ply their arts, develop their minds, drink a lot, like Miles—or little, like the Coes—or simply too much, like Martha.

New Leeds is broadly caricatured. Its "essence" is a "kind of exaggeration":

There were *three* village idiots, grinning, in the post office; the average winter resident who settled here had had three wives; there were eight young bohemians, with beards, leaning from their pickup trucks; twenty-one town drunkards. In wife-beating, child neglect, divorce, automobile accidents, falls, suicide, the town was on a sort of statistical rampage, like the highways on a holiday weekend.

There are no services in New Leeds. Livings are made from the summer people, and repairmen, like

tourists, vanish during the winter months. "Everything in the village was relentlessly running down,
buckling, warping, mildewing—including the human
beings." Keeping track of time is a practical challenge
for Martha. The Empire clock on the Sinnotts' mantel,
which the vicomte considers wrong for their "simple
cottage," gains ten minutes a day. Martha's watch loses
twenty, having been disabled when she went swim-
ming with it on the first week back in New Leeds, a
thing she had "never before in her life" done. In New
Leeds, neither people nor their machines function
normally.

Jane Coe is at home here. When the refrigerator is
out of order on the day of the party, she schemes to
avoid the labor of finding the repairman and persuad-
ing him to repair it. But her mind fills with images of
lugging in a block of ice, stashing it in the bathtub,
and chopping it by hand, and she decides that getting
the repairman will be easier. Finally, however, the
party goes on without ice. She was a "little bit embarrassed" the night Dolly Lamb came to dinner and they
were out of paper napkins, paper towels, and Kleenex
—Jane gave her linens to Martha—and had to use
toilet paper neatly folded by Warren, but he assures
her that such things do not matter. He and Jane agree
that it would be unfair to expect Jane to spend hours
ironing linen or washing delicate glassware or standing
over a hot stove. They prefer that she develop her
mind, but it is not clear that she spends the saved time
doing so.

Jane can override time, and she does. She has a
functioning alarm clock but nevertheless oversleeps on
the important morning of the play reading when she
has so much to do. She decides that the telegram announcing the death of Warren's mother might as well
be received the next day; after all, it is only by chance
that she picked up the mail today, and no one but the

Western Union man knows about the telegram. It is possible that he is "old-fashioned" and "conscientious" enough to check whether the Coes have gotten the message, and he must be forestalled. Jane can do that by answering the telegram—Warren will appreciate her thoughfulness—and wording the reply "so that it could sound as if it had been sent tomorrow, in case Warren ever saw it, and at the same time . . . fix it so that the Western Union man will not wonder." By means of a sleight-of-word and a night letter she solves the problem: tomorrow will be today when it arrives, she explains to the indifferent Western Union man. Even that ultimate fruit of time, death, can't spoil her fun.

Some day, she decided, she would tell [Warren] what she had gone through this morning, and they would laugh about it together; it would become one of Jane's exploits. "Do you remember the time your mother died?" she could hear herself begin, and her face, in the car mirror, at once assumed a sheepish bad-girl look.

Serious, thoughtful Dolly Lamb—a doll, a lamb, the sort of person who could be friends with both Martha and Sandy—attempts to come to terms with New Leeds through Sandy Gray. She is a forerunner of the proper Dottie of *The Group*, and in her efforts not to be shocked, she provides some of the funnier scenes in the book.

Her loyal support of Sandy's custody suit is based on truth of a kind; but though he is "gentle," attuned to nature, and capable of teaching children valuable lessons, she is not sure that his drinking *is* "social," his cooking frequent enough to feed children properly, his temper even enough to rear them well. Clover, on the other hand, has a way with children. Her housekeeping is slovenly, as Sandy's lawyer triumphantly establishes, but Clover's lawyer shows that the stan-

dards of the community prevail. Sandy's lawyer has
relied heavily upon the cleaning woman's testimony
that men's clothing hangs in Clover's closet, but on the
stand, the woman gleefully points out that Clover
wears men's clothing herself. Things are not, of course,
always what they seem, but in New Leeds it is hard
to make out even what they *seem*. Dolly's relief that
her dramatic testimony does not win Sandy's case is
well founded. As a matter of fact, Sandy's favorite
theories of child-rearing promote peanut butter and
prohibit shoes. Unfortunately, there has been a failure
of communication between him and a teacher who
requested that his son go shod to school. Sandy assumed that some pointless rule was at the bottom of
the request, but actually the other children were
throwing knives at the child's bare feet. Sandy is, in
short, a sorry lot, and Dolly's emotional investment in
him is as much a loss as her time and money.

The thing about New Leedsians, Martha says, is
that they do not work. The most vigorous activity
goes on in Miles's study, "lined with bookcases and
filing cases" and containing a "strange black bird, like
a raven" in a cage. Apprehensively approaching Miles
in this "eyrie," Warren assumes that Miles is observing
the bird's habits in connection with his recently developed interest in natural history. The villainous
Miles is dynamic, writing books, engendering babies,
instigating action, not impeded by scruples or honesty.
All-consuming and invulnerable, he is slightly removed from it all—he does not live in New Leeds—
and slightly above it all, in his tower room with his
silent, ravenlike bird, his needs well served by his near-
perfect wife:

She could take his abrupt dictation and decipher his manu-
script notes and hold the dinner till midnight if he did not
feel like eating. She could keep the child quiet in the morning when he had been sleeping a binge off. When they read

Aeschylus together . . . she looked up the hard words in the dictionary. . . . She kept the household accounts and never bothered him about money. If he felt like talking, she listened and asked intelligent questions. . . . She did not stimulate him—that was her only drawback.

Miles is Olympian in his grand disregard of the petty facts which encumber ordinary human beings and in his sweeping effect on other lives.

Dolly Lamb comes to New Leeds to work. In the course of events, Miles decides to sponsor a magazine article which will "discover" Warren Coe's art, to be written by Sandy Gray. The last time we see Dolly, who has no ready cash to lend Martha because she just "lent" Sandy $500, she has practically quit painting and is writing a first draft of the article on Warren, to get Sandy started. He will later "go over it and put in the ideas," she explains. But even the article is doomed, if by nothing else, by Warren's quarrel with Miles.

Warren works. The question of whether his work is brilliant or absurd is unanswered, and Warren is actually glad to renounce the opportunity to be publicly "discovered." He does not ask for recognition within his lifetime, and so, of course, he cannot fail— or succeed. Martha perceives that she has been avoiding the formal completion of her play out of fear that she had been merely "going through the motions of writing." All the toil which sets the artists apart from the rest of New Leeds comes to very little.

But Martha has seen the temptations and has resisted them; the play is almost finished when she sets out for the Coes' house. Martha knows New Leeds and has been describing it "for years now, with her gay, floating laugh, to incredulous outsiders who thought she was exaggerating." Thus she and John know that they "must be orderly and dignified; otherwise, they would surely go to pieces, like everybody else who came here."

Martha knows, too, her own weakness in dealing with Miles. While they were married, she yielded to his parsimony and let the workmen "stuff the wires back into the ceiling and just plaster over" the place where the dining room fixture had been. She was not "tight, exactly," but not sober either the night the fire broke out, and Miles was still quite drunk, "crashing around stupidly in the hedge, like a maddened buffalo, when firemen came." She withheld information about the wiring from the insurance company. Miles insisted that, since it was "normal practice" to cheat insurance companies, her impulse to tell the truth was really an impulse to destroy him. Theirs was the third house to catch fire that year; it was "as if she had lost . . . the principle of individuation and was simply a number in a series." She was also one of many New Leeds wives bullied and even beaten by their husbands.

There remains of that unsatisfactory past the foundation of the burnt house, which Martha and John pass every day; and Miles, not far away; and the gossip, which is based on some fact, even the part about her leaving a child. He was Miles's child, however, not hers. He died the next year. Martha has been unrealistically troubled by the thought that, had she remained with Miles, Barrett might have lived; she loved the little boy. She suffers, however, from a "clarity of mind" that becomes "more and more wearisome" to her. "Just as she was recalling, sadly, how she had grieved over Barrett's death, her memory tapped her sharply, like a teacher's ruler, and reminded her that she had not given Barrett a thought during the months when he must have been sickening; she had forgotten clean about him until she learned that he was dead." She half believes that Barrett is the reason she has been unable to have a child.

Martha's wearisome clarity of mind, love of truth, and devotion to order compel her to make distinc-

tions. Like Margaret Sargent, she values her honesty
and scruples. She is not guilt-ridden over having sub-
mitted to Miles; she would prefer not to have done so,
but the thing she hates is that she made a careless
mistake, like any New Leedsian, and failed to take
precautions. The sane New Leedsian would sidestep
the consequences and produce the baby as John's, but
Martha is not like that. Given the quality of her mind,
it is a straight but agonized road to the decision to
have an abortion. It would be easy to have the baby;
"the lawfulness of the whole picture had a special
charm for Martha." And the "obstacles in the path
were too great, the other way": she has no money, she
does not know an abortionist, and it will be difficult to
keep from involving John.

Yet all the while the moral part of Martha knew that she
would have to have an abortion because all her inclinations
were the other way. The hardest course was the right one;
in her experience, this was an almost invariable law. If her
nature shrank from the task, if it hid and cried piteously
for mercy, that was a sign that she was in the presence of
the ethical.

In deciding on an abortion, McCarthy says, Martha steps out of the charmed circle of immortality; her
death symbolizes the fact that she is mortal.[1] Other
characters in the novel are not subject to time. Jane
Coe can rearrange events in time; Miles revises the
past to justify himself; Dolly wastes her time with
impunity because she is not doing anything anyway;
Warren escapes time completely, substituting relativity in his painting and postponing judgment until after
his death. None of them changes with time, or builds
upon it, or invests in it.

Martha alone, with her malfunctioning chronome-
ters, is answerable to the terminable tickings of clocks,
the measurable durations of things. When John is late

getting home, when she cannot remember the date of her last period, it matters. The unchangeable past is as melancholy to contemplate as the ruins of the burned house. She could have prevented the fire, or she could have told the truth about it. Her scruples and honesty buckled under the weight of Miles and her self-doubts. At least now, while time is at hand, she can protect the future against another burden of guilt.

But as her creator says, in putting up a stake she forfeits immortality. The event that signals mortality is too perfunctorily arranged. Eleanor Considine comes suddenly, a goddess barreling along the road in a machine out of nowhere but the author's need for an appropriate way to kill off her heroine.

There are other flaws in the book, most notably perhaps the insubstantial character of John Sinnott, who seems to be important but about whom there is little to say. He is like an imaginary playmate to Martha, praising, criticizing, echoing, or contradicting her; he seems quite nice but hardly functional. The villainous Miles is more interesting and more imaginative; a high point of the book is the conversation, which he and Martha dominate, after the play reading. It relates to the novel's larger subjects; Jane picks at a spot on her skirt when the subject of the deaths of mothers comes up (she has withheld news of the death of Warren's mother), and, of course, what Miles has to say about Hamlet and the apparatus of cognition is to apply directly to Martha when she makes a decision that no sane New Leedsian would make.

The characters are all—save John—well realized, both in themselves and in relationship to the design of the book. Dolly Lamb and Warren Coe are complementary portraits of artists, her work lucid and over-disciplined and his obscure and experimental; both are tentative and isolated, however, confined within the cage of character and unlikely to break out. They

possess a sense of wonder, a responsiveness, and a reluctance to judge, and they are the natural victims of
people like Sandy Gray and Miles Murphy. They belong to the comic subplot.

The book is successful, too, in its portrayal of
Martha and the moral crisis of her life. It is perhaps
well to point out that this novel is not a feminist or
proabortionist polemic. Martha is feminine in a way
that offends latter-day feminists; she even "obeyed"
her first husband, though of course that was part of
the regrettable past. In her relationship with John she
wants "nothing to be hidden from him, not even the
bad parts of her nature. She respected his privacy,
because he was a man, but for herself, if she could not
be transparent, she did not want to love." McCarthy
refers to the over-thirty females in the novel as "girls."
And the question which Martha must answer is not
whether abortion is right or wrong, or whether she
should be free to have one; the abortion of years ago is
not part of the past that she regrets. The question is
whether bearing a child of uncertain paternity is right
or wrong under these circumstances. Martha considers
it wrong, and the important thing is that she acts out
of moral conviction rather than uncertainty and weakness. Making the decision is less difficult than gathering the courage and resourcefulness to act upon it,
than overcoming the inertia by which one is tempted
to repeat oneself and claim a spot within the charmed
circle.

In discussing *A Charmed Life*, one might again
take issue with the use of the word "novel" in a strict
sense. McCarthy is not sure that the book is a novel
because of the fairy-tale element—the exaggerated
portrayal of New Leeds and the "symbolic" function
of Martha's death. A novel by McCarthy's definition
in "The Fact in Fiction" (*On the Contrary*) is a
"prose book of a certain thickness that tells a story of

real life." Its prose and its commitment to "the empiric element in experience" distinguish it from other books of a certain thickness. It is set not in heaven or Lilliput or the future but in the present world, where beasts do not talk and the devil does not appear. Not, McCarthy adds, that there is anything wrong with a story in which beasts talk; it is simply not a novel.

We not only make believe we believe a novel, but we do substantially believe it, as being continuous with real life, made of the same stuff, and the presence of fact in fiction, of dates and times and distances, is a kind of reassurance—a guarantee of credibility. If we read a novel, say, about conditions in post-war Germany, we expect it to be an accurate report. . . .

A novel is full of places and people and things, of facts, of news, of gossip and scandal; the part that does not exist in time and space does not violate possibility.

Even given this broad definition, one still, of course, cannot say whether a prose book is a story or stories, but a point of interest is that what some critics consider a weakness of McCarthy's fiction—her fondness for details—is rooted in her theory. *The Group* has been damned by some as little more than a catalogue of fashionable things and ideas in the 1930s. *Birds of America* has offended readers who deplore what they regard as the subordination of ideas to trivia. But the emphasis on the materials of life in McCarthy's fiction is based on moral as well as aesthetic considerations.

I have said that one of the strengths of *Memories of a Catholic Girlhood* is its richness of detail. Whether McCarthy's view of her early life as so often a struggle against the ugly, the common, and the humiliating is cause or effect of personality is a matter of her psychology, which is not our subject. Her critics sometimes call her a snob, however, and one reason is her reliance not only on manners but on taste and appearance, on style, if you will, as indicators of character. What we remember about Henry Mulcahy (*The Groves of Academe*) is not just the viciousness of his mind but the personal unattractiveness of the man and even of his house, smelling of urine from diapers drying on the radiators—things that are not of the essence.

McCarthy recalls that as a very young child she had "a passionate love of beauty"; she disliked ugly people and resisted the idea that "anyone beautiful could be bad." The ugliness that bewildered and repelled her as she grew older was elective. The shabby sewing room that was good enough for the children when they visited the McCarthys, their own dismal house, shabby clothing, and tasteless diet—these things were chosen for them. To McCarthy, such a choice poses a mystery if it does not argue outright a moral deficiency.

The young Mary, critical of Aunt Margaret's food and even her "hideous" flowers—"golden glow and sickly nasturtiums"—and the teenager, puzzled by the Bents' house in Montana, have much in common with McCarthy's fictional heroines. Margaret Sargent likes what she perceives as the connoisseur in Mr. Breen and basks in a "sense of ritualistic 'rightness' " in his compartment furnished with his leather luggage and attended by a white-coated waiter. Martha Sinnott's immaculate glassware and linens and Rosamund Brown's cakes made from scratch reveal the kinship of these characters to each other and to their creator. This insistence on the forms and ceremonies of life is carried to another generation in Rosamund Brown's son, scrubbing away at the filthy toilets of his Paris quarters and reflecting at length on the philosophical and sociological implications of both their condition and his efforts to improve it.

Such fastidiousness is not devoid of something

that can be called snobbishness, but it is not entirely, or even chiefly, snobbish. It is consistent with, and essential to, the humanistic strain—the Preston love of the "rule of law"—that pervades McCarthy's work. She believes in the importance of what Irvin Stock calls " 'appearances'—the . . . concrete facts of what one is and does."[2]

The point is explicit in *The Group*. While the girls are still in college, there is an argument about the "meaning" of Cézanne's still lifes. Lakey says that the important thing is the formal arrangement of shapes; Norine holds that the point is the *spirit* of the apples. With disdain for appearances McCarthy has no patience, and Norine's own "forms"—her apartment, her clothing, her ungroomed body—imply the squalor of the girl's "essence." There is no excuse for slovenliness —physical, mental, or moral.

5

.~.

A Brave New Generation:
The Group

The Group is about eight Vassar graduates, class of
1933, who got together in college to reserve the South
Tower for themselves. The novel begins with their
first wedding, a week after commencement, and ends
with their first funeral, seven years later, in the same
Episcopal church on Stuyvesant Square in New York
City. The central figure in both ceremonies is Kay
Leiland Strong Petersen, the boldest and most unconventional member of the Group, the only westerner
(from Salt Lake City), and always, to some extent, an
outsider, not "born into the Social Register" or into
great wealth.

The girls emerge from Vassar perceiving themselves as a "different breed . . . from the languid buds
of the previous decade." They take the privileges and
responsibilities of their class and education seriously;
they are interested in politics and social reform. Although only Polly really has to, they all expect to
work, at volunteer jobs if necessary. At Kay's wedding, they take inventory of themselves:

Libby MacAusland had a promise from a publisher; Helena
Davison, whose parents, out in Cincinnati, no, Cleveland,
lived on the income of their income, was going into teaching . . . Polly Andrews . . . was to work as a technician
in the new Medical Center; Dottie Renfrew was slated for
social work in a Boston settlement house; Lakey was off to

Paris to study art history . . . Pokey Prothero, who had
been given a plane for graduation, was getting her pilot's
license so as to be able to commute three days a week to
Cornell Agricultural School [to study veterinary medi-
cine], and . . . Priss Hartshorn . . . had simultaneously an-
nounced her engagement to a young doctor and landed a
job with the N.R.A.

Their determination to be a "different breed"
finds ceremonial expression in Kay's wedding. The
others have been skeptical during the courtship. Harald Petersen's egotistical and breezy letters and long
silences made them fear that Kay was deceived in him.
But he is not, after all, "of their own background,"
and they know the "unwisdom of making large judgments from one's own narrow little segment of experience." Enlightened by their Vassar education, they
resist class-based prejudices, like the common one
against theater people—Harald works as a stage man-
ager while preparing to make his mark as a playwright
—and their open-mindedness is justified when the
marriage actually takes place. They claim it as a "point
for their side that the iconoclast and scoffer was the
first of the little band to get married."

To be sure, they have misgivings—about the
bride's black hat, the groom's black suede shoes, the
absence of parents or "*any older person*," the fact that
Kay has already lived with Harald—but the very
awkwardness of the little ceremony becomes a virtue
upon their recollection that Kay and Harald are "too
busy and dynamic to let convention cramp their style."
Only Elinor Eastlake, the enigmatic beauty who has
from the beginning dominated and fascinated the rest
of the Group, regards the affair as humiliating and
considers Kay a "*cruel, ruthless, stupid* person who
was marrying Harald for ambition." She says little,
however, and the others do not notice the irony of her
distributing bags of rice to throw at the newlyweds as

they depart, via subway, for their honeymoon at Coney Island.

Two days later Lakey leaves for Europe. During her long absence, occasional recollections of Lakey—remote, intelligent, of irreproachable integrity unsullied by compassion—remind the others of their own imperfections. They always wanted her approval; seven years later, when they assemble to meet her at the dock, they still do. War has broken out in Europe, and she is coming home. They are afraid that she will find them provincial and dull.

Indeed, they are a little stodgy. Dottie, the Bostonian, never worked at the settlement house. A few days after Kay's wedding, that "serene and conventional" young woman astonished Kay and Harald with the announcement that she had taken a lover. The affair had a very short duration; it is, as a matter of fact, one of the most explicitly described one-night stands in all of literature and one of the most notorious. But for several years now, Dottie has been respectably married to a very wealthy man.

Polly, whose family lost their money in the crash of 1929, supported herself by working as a medical technician. She had an unhappy love affair which was ending when her father came to live with her. After years of being afflicted by "melancholia," her father had discovered that he was manic-depressive and felt that he was due a period of the manic phase of his illness; the attendant extravagance strained Polly's income. But Polly's is a story of virtue rewarded—she is a sensible and likable young woman—for she married a young physician who even wanted her father to live with them. Now they have a little girl.

Priss, after a time, gave up her job to devote her energy to motherhood. She misses her work and remains interested in politics, favoring the Roosevelt administration and involving herself in the effort to

get America into the war to save Europe. Her Republican husband is an ambitious young pediatrician, and
Priss very carefully trains her son according to the
best modern theories.

The wealthiest member of the Group, Pokey, is
least in evidence. At last report, she was still studying
to be a veterinarian; she married, incongruously, the
others feel, a poet who seems to have tenure as a graduate student at Princeton, and they have twins. Plump,
messy, insensitive—she has no sense of smell—Pokey is
exempt from the thousand natural shocks that ordinary flesh is heir to.

Helena, also very rich, perhaps the most sensible
and certainly the most ironic of the Group, abandoned
her plan to work at an experimental school. The others wonder whether she was bribed by her father's
offer of a trip to Europe, but she was probably swayed
by his argument that she should not take a job that
some other girl might need. Helena remains unmarried, a wry and not unsympathetic observer of the
activities of the others.

Libby, insincere, gossipy, a *mauvaise fille* in Lakey's judgment, is the only one of the Group actually
to make her mark. After a period of unsuccessfully
reviewing books for a publishing company, falsely
representing herself as impoverished and in need of
the work, she made it as a literary agent's assistant.
Now married to an author of best-selling historical
novels, she leads a glamorous life.

Kay went to work in personnel at Macy's. As
often as not, she was the breadwinner for herself and
Harald, who never held a job for long. Loyally, she
promoted the legend of his genius in spite of his cru-
elty to her and their frequent quarrels. When she finally had to recognize that his failings, professional
and personal, could not be explained away, the marriage came to violence and to an end. Seven years

after graduation, divorced and jobless, Kay is staying at the Vassar Club, staked by her Dads. She has taken up the cause of American preparedness for the war.

They all show up to meet Lakey. As they wait for her to finish with Customs, it gradually dawns on them in what sense the baroness accompanying her is Lakey's friend; it even occurs to them that Lakey, always "frightening and superior," will "look down on them for not being Lesbians." The reunion is, however, very warm. The others soon learn to treat Maria as another husband, included in gatherings which include husbands, otherwise not. Disturbing as the situation seems at first, it works out very well, and members of the Group see each other from time to time over the next few months.

Then, in July, while "airplane-spotting" from her window at the Vassar Club, Kay falls to her death, and the Group must arrange the funeral because her parents cannot get to New York in time. Helena's mother calls Kay the first American war casualty, and radio announcements on the progress of the war in Europe punctuate the proceedings as, with assistance from two of their mothers, some members of the Group attend to Kay's laying out in Helena's apartment. They do what they can to make the funeral what Kay would have wanted. Afterward, on the way to the cemetery with Harald, Lakey avenges Kay. Harald boasts of his abuse of Kay and claims kinship with Lakey as a fellow "superior" being, but, fascinated, he is finally compelled to ask: "Did you sleep with her?" "Lakey smiled, like a lizard. 'You ought to have asked Kay. . . . She was such an honest girl at the end.' " His outburst—"You're rotten. . . . Did you corrupt the whole group?"—satisfies her. She has "forced this dreadful man at last to be truthful," to reveal the conventional limits of his vaunted unconventionality.

The Group is a large and complex novel, with

events spanning seven years and eight characters in
their relationships with parents, lovers, husbands, and
friends. The organization is chronological, with some
departures: the account of Lakey's arrival from Italy
is a flashback at Kay's funeral. The narrative point of
view changes; third-person throughout, sometimes the
story is carried by the voice of the Group in a kind of
chorus, sometimes of several girls, sometimes of one.
Occasionally it is that of a mother, or, in one extended
passage, of Hatton, Pokey's family's butler, who is,
McCarthy says, a kind of stand-in for Pokey's mother.
As the point of view changes, so does the manner.
Helena's wry irony informs the description of the
apartment occupied by Norine Schmittlapp, the "political" Vassar classmate who is not a member of the
Group:

Every item in it seemed to be saying something, pontificat-
ing: Norine and Put were surrounded by articles of belief,
down to the last can of evaporated milk and the single,
monastic pillow on the double bed. It was different from
Kay's apartment, where the furniture was only asking to
be admired or talked *about*. But here, in this dogmatic lair,
nothing had been admitted that did not make a "relevant
statement," though what the polar bear [rug] was saying
Helena could not make out.

Libby's dishonesty and affectation show through
her contemplation of Polly's living arrangement:

. . . the quaint life of Polly's rooming house was all very
well to dilate on to other girls . . . but a man would think,
to hear about it, still more to see it in the flesh, that you
were desperate for company if you had to fall back on
that. . . . What was it about those roomers, about the
brownstone house itself, the very carpet on the stairs . . .
that Libby's feminine instinct told her would cook a girl's
goose with any normal member of the opposite sex? . . .
It would . . . be all right, strangely enough, for Libby to

live in that house, not that she would: she could say she was gathering material for a story. . . .

Helena is cool, detached, observant—a reliable and intelligent, if not unbiased, witness. Libby thinks in ill-chosen clichés and refers everything to her admiring notion of herself—also a cliché. We can never put much stock in what Libby thinks. The changing voices are an important means of individualizing characters; as much as the Group have in common, they are fully differentiated.

The novel is full of details. Discussing its impact on the literary world, Doris Grumbach remarks that "the whole shape of the book, and its intention, were destined to be lost in the flood of its details: social, economic, psychiatric, sexual, medical, and domestic."[1] Enormously popular, it was widely condemned, Grumbach observes, as trivial, as sensational, even as "flatly written and incoherently structured."

Many such criticisms were based on a rather casual reading of the novel and failed to take into account its intention or to understand the narrative voices employed. Even a more sympathetic reader may grant, however, that the novel is flawed. The inclusion of the butler Hatton is, for example, hard to justify even as an overelaborate metaphor of the insulating powers of great wealth. He is nonetheless a joy to meet. He manages the Protheros' affairs, from seeing to it that Pokey goes to college to attending Kay's funeral as a representative of the older Protheros. Hatton gave up his plan of returning to England after he "did the distinguished thing of losing all he had in the stock-market crash," while the coarser Mr. Porthero recovered from a small setback and then went through the Depression getting richer. The family depend upon Hatton because they are "dim-witted and vain of it, as a sign of good breeding."

But Hatton is his own story, not part of the Group's. McCarthy frequently publishes parts of her novels first as short stories, and there are often short stories embedded in the novels. In general, however, *The Group* integrates its diverse materials and interweaves the stories into a unified whole, which McCarthy uses as a vehicle for comedy and satire and as a means of exploring—to use Irvin Stock's words again —"how hard it has been for intellectuals in our time to behave decently and humanely."[2]

The Group especially believe in social progress, and they desire not "to become like Mother and Daddy, stuffy and frightened." As a matter of fact, their parents are less stuffy at times than are their daughters. The mothers of Dottie, Priss, and Helena are in evidence, and so is Polly's father; according to McCarthy, the mothers were an even larger part of the original plan than of the finished work. The mothers have more resilience and imagination than the daughters; they are more substantial. The girls are uncomfortable about their absence from Kay's wedding and relieved to have them help with the funeral.

The Group's experiments in modern ways are unsatisfying. Dottie tries out sexual freedom with an indifferent but candid young man, a divorced friend of the classless Harald. But for all the etiquette surrounding the contraceptive equipment and for all the sociological importance of the brief "affair," the purely sexual relationship is no more rewarding for a sensitive young woman in 1933 than in 1903. Dottie continues to yearn for Dick, but it is a "languid bud" of the previous generation, her mother, whose impulse it is to postpone Dottie's wedding when she learns about Dick. "Mrs. Renfrew was aware of the oddity of this situation, in which . . . the daughter was hurrying herself into a 'suitable' marriage while the mother was pleading with her to seek out an unsuitable rake."

We see little of Dottie after her marriage, but we see a good deal of Priss as matron, chiefly in her role as mother. Sloan, her pediatrician husband, directs the rearing of their baby from the comfortable distance of the theorist. Mrs. Hartshorn is bemused that her daughter breast-feeds the infant. In an earlier day, she observes, "We swore by the bottle, we of the avant-garde. . . . First we nursed our babies; then science told us not to. Now it tells us we were right in the first place. Or were we wrong then but would be right now?" Immunities and benefits of cuddling notwithstanding, Priss's milk is inadequate to Stephen's needs, and she is haunted for years by the sound of the interminably wailing infant voice telling her down the hospital corridor that the feedings are too scant and too far apart, regardless of the evidence of a satisfactory weight gain. She resists a nagging fear that her ambitious husband is sacrificing her and their baby to an experiment in child care and remains faithful to the progressive philosophy.

Measured by his standards, she is a successful mother in every area but one, and there she and her son come to an impasse: at two-and-a-half, he still resists toilet training. She secretly believes that young Stephen is taking his revenge for the hunger of his infancy and the austere regimentation of his life.

Rigid adherence to the latest ideas of child psychology are as pointless as unquestioning faith in psychoanalysis, which we see through the sensible eyes of Polly Andrews. Polly's lover, Gus Leroy, left his wife, Esther, when he discovered that she was running around with a Party organizer. Gus is a Communist but "phlegmatic" in his political commitment and unreceptive to a "free relationship" in marriage. At Esther's direction, he is undergoing analysis to see whether the marriage can be saved, and Polly's affair with him drags on for a year while she waits for him to divorce Esther and marry her. To Polly's "naked eye" Gus seems entirely normal; as far as she can see, the "only thing wrong with him was that he was spending $25 a week going to a psychoanalyst."

Finally, as Gus prepares Polly to send him back to Esther—he lacks the volition to simply go—the truth comes out. Gus is "blocked." He never dreams, and so he has nothing to tell his analyst. Polly objects to the doctor's charging for hour after hour of silence, but in an exquisite variation of Catch 22, Gus explains that his silence "shows the treatment is working and I'm fighting it." Polly is left to conclude that Gus is "ordinary. That was what was the matter with him." The ordinariness is, of course, the quality of mind which accepts the idea that he needs psychoanalysis because he objects to his wife's infidelity, which swallows "modern" ideas whole in disregard of all common sense.

Nevertheless, the break with Gus is painful. The pain is eased by the arrival of Polly's refreshingly mad father, who, for all his ruinous extravagance, is much more fun than Gus and by no means ordinary. After all these years, he and Polly's mother are calling it quits just as Gus is returning to a particularly unpleasant modern marriage. Mr. Andrews, a Trotskyite, is more imaginative even in his politics than that ordinary Stalinist, Gus; and more *right*, Polly thinks with satisfaction. He knows a hawk from a handsaw.

There are various political threads in the novel, but the burden of leftist political activism is borne chiefly by Harald Petersen and Norine Schmittlapp. Harald foresees a brave new world of abundance and leisure, with artists and technicians (his class) rising to the top. Kay is very proud of him as a "social thinker." For her own part, she is not "really strong for the idea of equality," and she has trouble remembering that her class is finished. When Harald explains it all to

Dottie, Kay helps him impress her friend by mention-
ing, as a sign of the dawn of a better society, the
"smart new renovated tenements. . . ." Of course, the
rents are high, but look what you get. The renovation
projects are carried out by capitalists, but Harald believes that capital has a part to play in the short run.
Dottie plunges him into gloom by asking what happened to the poor former inhabitants of the tenements, a question for which Harald has no answer.
Answers are not essential, however, for one as "para-
doxical" as Harald, who "would whirl around and attack the very things he believed in most." His ideas
are, as a matter of fact, very susceptible to attack.

Harald is active in the union movement. The year
after his marriage, he and Norine's husband, Putnam
Blake, lead a sympathy strike of guests in support of
the striking waiters at the Hotel Carlton Cavendish
(an event in which Dorothy Parker, Alexander
Woollcott, and Robert Benchley more notably partic-
ipated). The newspaper account of the strike and the
arrest of Harald and Put provides a kind of pivot near
the novel's center as characters read the news and
react to it, at the same time bringing us up to date in
their lives. Out in Cleveland, Mrs. Davison studies the
accompanying photograph and shrewdly remarks to
Helena that Norine "has probably got Putnam Blake
and Harald wound around her little finger." In New
York, Hatton, in the line of his duty of reading the
paper for the Protheros, shows the story to Pokey's
mother, and the poor lady is stricken ill by the recollection that Harald has been entertained in her house:
"A jailbird!" Up in Boston, Dottie's mother tells Dottie about the incident and starts a discussion which
leads to Dottie's telling her mother about Harald's
friend, Dick, all the way to "He made me . . . go to a
doctor and get a contraceptive, one of those diaphragm things. . . ."

Mrs. Renfrew was stunned; her wide bright eyes canvassed her daughter's face, as if trying to reassemble her. "Perhaps that's the modern way," she finally ventured.

The modern way is crude and formless among the likes of Harald and his friends. The whole matter of the sympathy strike would be more to their credit if it were not for the report that drinks consumed before the walkout were not paid for.

But Harald and Norine are villains. More destructive than Jane Coe, less intelligent than Henry Mulcahy, they belong to the same class of self-servers, the chaos of their lives a constant danger to everything they touch, from social causes to other people's lives. Miles Murphy, too, is villainous, but I exclude him from this company because of his achievements—the others accomplish nothing except the indulgence of their natures—and because one can imagine enjoying his company in spite of his faults.

During the first year of Kay's marriage, Helena witnesses, at a party, a furtive embrace between Norine and Harald. The next day she unwillingly accepts Norine's invitation to the apartment where Norine and Put live amid dirty dishes, bookcases made of orange crates, black walls, canned goods, and a polar bear rug. So much is visible to Helena's unaided eye, but Norine displays also the furnishings of her sordid mind, attributing her adulterous affair to her envy of the "sexual superiority" of the Group, to Harald's being a better bridge player than Put, to Put's impotence, and so on. With whores, Put can perform; but with a good woman—i.e., Norine—he cannot. It is too much for Helena, who finally advises Norine:

You say your husband can't sleep with you because you're a "good woman." I suggest you enlighten him. Tell him what you do with Harald. And about the progressive-school teacher with the wife and six children. That ought to get his pecker up. And have him take a look at this apartment. And at the ring around your neck. If a man slept with you, you'd leave a ring around him. Like your bathtub.

Norine listens with interest for a time, but she is ir-redeemable. She is reminded of the argument over Cézanne's apples. "You're hipped on forms," she tells Helena, "while I'm concerned with meanings."

Cleaning up the apartment. . . . Buying toilet paper, buying Clorox, buying a new dress. Notice your stress on bour-geois acquisition, on mere *things*. . . . You don't touch on the basic things. The intangibles.

Norine is forever showing up. Five years later when Priss runs into her, Norine's "forms" have undergone a change. She is married again, to a rich Jew, and living in a "classical modern" house with a staff of servants and a new "passion," comparative religion. Her "cerebralism" still distracts her from the mun-dane, however, and she cannot handle servants, a de-fect that she considers a "relic" of her political past. The "essence" of Norine is captured in the scene in which the butler brings in a tray containing a tar-nished silver pot with coffee cups, cream, and sugar wrapped in paper marked "Schrafft's."

I can't get used to being rich. . . . I always take the sugar they give you home with me. . . . But the help can't be bothered to unwrap them.

Neither in her political past nor in her religious present does the intangible of friendship with Kay prevent Norine's continuing her affair with Harald, although he has tired of her sexually and the betrayal of Kay now takes place at a different level. Norine was active in the disastrous events which led to Kay's commitment to a mental hospital. She tells Priss about how she "cleared up a few points" for the doctors. She

explained Kay's hostility to her as based in a lesbian
attachment.

But a lot of basic things were the matter. Sex. Competitive-
ness with men. . . . Thwarted social strivings. . . . And all
the time she was driving [Harald] to make money, she was
ruthlessly undercutting him because of her penis-envy. Plus
a determination to punish him for not giving her a vicari-
ous success. . . .

Poor Kay. What chance could she have against all
that cerebralism? From Norine, we might be disin-
clined to believe that the doctors listened to her about
Kay's condition, but by now we have already seen one
interviewing Kay at the hospital, and he is not to be
trusted. Indeed, the only trustworthy psychiatrist
around is Polly's husband, Jim Ridgeley, who went
into psychiatry because he thought it was a science
and now is getting out of it because it is not.

Kay took Animal Behavior at Vassar, and she likes
to analyze people, too, particularly to rationalize Harald's failings; but he is competent to do that himself,
and Norine is a better assistant than Kay because she
has no relationship to truth. Kay was not always
truthful; that was one of the things that used to bother
the others in the Group. She confesses to Jim Ridgeley that she used to lie, but never to discredit anyone.
She was, however, as Lakey says, very honest *at the
end*. Reasoning from the fact of Kay's death and from
what McCarthy says about the mortality of the heroine, Ruth Mathewson recalls that at Vassar Lakey
liked Kay because she was "malleable" and "capable of
learning," that Kay was a "blurter" who liked games
of Truth. "In the great classical tradition, she winds
up in a madhouse, where the mad may be sane and the
sane mad."[3]

But Kay *develops* truthfulness; it is a thing that
she learns. Harald, too, saw Kay as educable, or at least

he expected, he wrote to his father, to give "form and direction" to her "vitality." He failed to do precisely that, but he was instrumental in her growth in another way. "Harald isn't very truthful," she tells Jim, "and I've had a reaction against that." She has had to learn the truth about Harald and with it the truth about herself. In the hospital, she decides that her grief is

for a Harald-That-Never-Was, not for the real Harald. But if she lost the real Harald, who was not such a much-ness, she lost her only link with the Harald-That-Never-Was. Then it was really finished—her dream. . . . There was something else. She had always despised failures, but if Harald had left her, she was one.

She has, she realizes, "tried to bind [Harald] with possessions." But things do not matter to him.

The novel has prompted many a contemptuous observation about its domestic details—its recipes and furnishings, from Harald's spaghetti to Polly's pâté, laboriously sieved, buttered, brandied, sherried; from Norine's lair to Libby's "spiffy apartment" to Mrs. Davison's morning room. It is nearly four hundred pages long, however; McCarthy takes time and space to recreate an era and to create characters. She has been charged with writing talky novels, and there is a lot of talk in The Group. But if a novel is continuous with real life, both qualities are not only defensible but essential. Real people are surrounded by things, and they talk, externally and internally; in The Group, the details not only contribute to the reality of the novel but are part of its subject.

A lot of Kay's talk is about her acquisitions, including Harald, whose brilliance is one of her attributes, part of the success story that people back in Salt Lake City believe about her. Kay, like Margaret Sargent, has trouble coming to terms with things: her seams are crooked at her wedding, and she improvidently dies without a dress in suitable condition for her funeral. But unlike Norine, who regards her slovenliness and disorder as a mark of her superiority to the trivial, Kay requires nice things and ceremony and associates *them* with superiority. She is a terrible snob, too. At Vassar her friends felt that she failed to "realize the little social nuances," and they were embarrassed by her name-dropping and her representing "poor Harald" as a Yale man when he only went to graduate school at Yale. *They* accepted him as a "natural gentleman," of course, and were impressed by him, too, but that was not the point.

Kay has a "ruthless hatred of poor people." She knows that "subjectively, of course, she ought to pity" Harald's father, Anders, an Idaho teacher who worked up to principal, from which post he was dismissed when—"shades of Ibsen!"—he discovered "some funny business about the high-school bookkeeping." But actually she fears Anders and Harald's loyalty to him—one of Harald's few endearing qualities—because she feels that Harald is just "identifying with failure." As for his mother,

The sight of her . . . labored pencil recipes . . . made [Kay] cold and hard as nails. . . . she could not abide Harald's chile con carne, though it was still a big success with company, who did not know the source and thought it was something glamorous he had learned in the theatre. She had no doubt that [Harald's mother] used oleomargarine; she could see a white slab of it on their humble oilcloth with a cheap plated-silver butter knife (the kind you sent in coupons for) lying by its moist side!

At first, Kay admires Harald's culinary skills. His recipes are a big part of Harald's world, and the fact that he and Kay plan a sharing of domestic duties shows how modern they are. Harald "put garlic in everything and was accounted quite a cook." But for

most readers, he was discredited in the first chapter by
the punch at the wedding breakfast, a concoction of
applejack, maple syrup, lemon juice, and White Rock;
everyone agrees that the maple syrup makes "all the
difference." The girls are very much interested in
recipes for drinks, especially one made of equal parts
of gin, lemon juice, and grenadine. Not long past Shir-
ley Temples, they can easily be forgiven a taste for
drinks that sound as if they should be frozen with
sticks in them; and Harald can surely be forgiven for
showing off before such an appreciative audience.
"Where did you get this *man?*" they cry. But the
reader will not easily be misled thereafter by rumors
of Harald's gourmet cuisine.

"Listen to how Harald fixes chipped beef"; "You
ought to get your cook to try the new way of fixing
canned beans," Kay proudly advises her friend from
Boston. "It sounds terribly good," Dottie agrees, "but
Daddy would die."

Harald nodded. He began to talk, very learnedly, about the
prejudice that existed in conservative circles against canned
goods. . . . Modern machinery and factory processes, of
course, had eliminated all danger of bacteria, and yet the
prejudice lingered, which was a pity, since many canned
products, like vegetables picked at their peak and some of
the Campbell soups, were better than anything the home
cook could achieve.

The key word is "better." Dismissing the universal experience of mankind as conservative prejudice,
Harald assumes a superior posture as enlightened
promoter of modern technology, all on the basis of his
soup-drenched meatloafs. Depression fare, as Mathewson observes,[4] but a nutritious expedient for working
people without much time or money.

Kay's mother's "cheaper" recipes, sent for in a
spirit of friendly competition, call for cooking sherry

and mushrooms, ramekins and lettuce cups, shrimps and alligator pear in lime gelatin. Cooking sherry and lime Jello are not gourmet staples, but Prohibition was in effect until 1933 and even Polly uses canned consommé; yet the truth is that neither Kay nor Harald is much of a cook. Kay laboriously follows recipes, thus making cooking "academic and lifeless" according to the more freewheeling Harald, but she routinely adds fifteen minutes' cooking time.

In just three months' time, the little differences multiply and intensify. At first, Kay was

Harald's echo. But now if he said why not be sensible and open a can . . . she would scream that she could not do that, it might be all right for him, but she could not live that way, week in, week out, eating like an animal, just to keep alive.

By now, Harald's schedule is so erratic that he cannot even show up for dinner at a predictable hour, let alone cook it. Kay does all the shopping and cooking. She likes the ritual of a cocktail before dinner, but Harald drinks too much, and that worries her. She insists on an expensive apartment and suffers the disapproval of Norine and Put in their $40-a-month basement. She serves real cream "as a matter of course."

She is living beyond her means, for her resources are severely limited. Even her genius husband looks for all the world like a quarrelsome ne'er-do-well, superficially intelligent, always just missing success because somebody had it in for him. Yet Kay goes on believing in his brilliant promise. When he has a moment of near success, she celebrates with a party and proudly shows the Group her apartment. It is very modern, with white walls, blond furniture, and steel lamps.

There were no rugs yet and, instead of curtains, only white Venetian blinds. . . . Instead of flowers, they had ivy. . . .

instead of a bed, they had a big innerspring mattress with another mattress on top of it. . . .

The voice here is of the other girls; in the awareness of what is missing (rugs, curtains, flowers, a bed) sounds a note, perhaps, of those diehard class prejudices. But there are too many "instead of's" in Kay's life. Instead of a devoted husband, she has the faithless Harald.

"God, how that man suffered!" Norine says to Priss. Confiding in Lakey after the funeral, Harald too sees himself as long-suffering, with the peculiar reasoning that McCarthy's worst villains apply from a premise of total self-acceptance. It was, he explains, Kay's "unreasonable" jealousy that "wrecked everything in the end."

I never gave her anything to be jealous of. I protected her. Whenever I slept with a woman, I made sure Kay could never find out. That meant I could never break clean with them. No matter how fed up I was.

Citing Norine as example—"For years I had to keep her hoping, so that she wouldn't be moved to tell Kay"—he remarks bitterly, "Christ, I was only seeing her for Kay's sake."

The beauty of the story is that what Norine has told Priss corroborates its broad outline; the only question is just what kind of service Harald was doing Kay by sleeping with Norine to begin with. His infidelity is a given, so far from being a vice as to become the occasion for virtue. *Kay* is the one made to feel guilty. Describing the events of the crucial night to Polly, Kay says that Harald accused her of "insane jealousy."

I had sunk so low as to suspect my best friend. . . . Well, I did feel rather cheap, though I hadn't meant sex. I'd never suspect Harald of sleeping with Norine—she's not Harald's type.

Naturally it was the "political" Norine who arranged Kay's admission to a hospital for a rest and a chance to think, away from Harald; she couldn't afford a hotel, but Blue Cross would pay for the hospitalization. And Harald, for whatever reason, simply committed her as a mental patient. After she faces the truth in the hospital, we do not see Kay up close again. We hear reports that she went home for a year, that she divorced Harald, that she lost her job and consequently her apartment because of her confinement in a mental hospital. "Her whole house of cards," Priss says sadly. But Kay saw that it *was* a house of cards, not habitable for an honest girl. The Kay-That-Never-Was is a failure.

Priss is a failure, too. Sloan is cruel and insensitive, and his blueprint for little Stephen's life is oppressive; Priss can see that, but she does not act upon her own good sense. She distrusts herself. Nervous, embarrassed, doubting, Priss can go on forever obeying Sloan's orders. She regrets having given up her job and her social ideals for him, and she believes that he too would be happier if she had not done so. But she does not apply the obvious lesson. Kay does, and that is the difference.

The Group is grounded in the discrepancy between the expectations of the graduates who attend Kay's wedding and the attainments of the women who attend her funeral. Kay epitomized the promise of a modern way of life, free from stifling conventions, cutting across class barriers, equipped with the best new ideas. They admired her plans when she married Harald. To be sure, they kept a little distance; none of them offered a house or an apartment or a club for the reception, and they felt a little guilty about it. But they do not stint on the funeral. Kay is laid out in a Fortuny dress bought by Lakey and buried in a grave donated by Pokey to rest in style "among all those

Livingstons and Schuylers." Lakey is surprised by a
tear during the ceremony; "the sole emotion she had
willed herself to feel was the cold fierce passion that
this funeral should be perfect, a flawless mirror of
what Kay would find admirable."

If, in 1940, Lakey is "more human" than the others remembered, so are they all as they bury the hopes
of their youth. The only sour notes are Norine, who
shows up wearing her infant, Ichabod, in a sling "to
give him the experience of death," and Harald, who
arrives late and creates a small disturbance, thus pro-
voking Helena to think that he is "taking the joy out
of Kay's funeral." These two, however, no longer
matter. The Group close around Kay, and Lakey ban-
ishes Harald even from the past by allowing him to
draw the false conclusion that, in his illiberal mind,
makes the past unthinkable.

Mailer complains that nothing happens to the
Group, that they never break out of the cage of their
character.[5] But things do happen to them. They grow
older, they marry, they have children. Polly has an
affair; Libby is nearly raped; Kay is committed to a
mental hospital; Lakey settles down with a female
lover. They don't do much—that is the point. It is not
the nature of mankind to break out of the cage of
character—that, too, is the point. But one of the
Group does.

The women who come to meet Lakey are eager
to show her their apartments, their husbands, their
children, "except Kay, who had nothing to show her
but who therefore felt she had the best claim on her."
Kay is still bold, still a "blurter." She is the first to
understand that Lakey and Maria are lovers, and the
others, uncertain how to act in this modern instance,
turn "by instinct" to her for leadership. She is the
only one who claims to be able to picture "with
equanimity" the embraces of the lovers; the others

come to like Maria "as a person" but remain troubled by her relationship with their friend: "if only she could have finished in a tail, like a mermaid!"

Kay sounds perfectly natural, in short, and not in the least chastened and subdued. She is looking for a job and has an appointment for an interview with Saks. There has been some discussion by critics of her death as a possible suicide, but there is no reason to think that it is. The two characters who bring up the subject are Harald and Libby, but Harald wants to think that Kay killed herself just to show *him* and thus regain his centrality in Kay's affairs, and Libby always has a gossip-mongering, prurient interest in human events. We have not paid attention to the novel if we believe anything either of them says. The others accept the death as accidental, and the evidence points toward an accident. It seems an artistic imperative that a "symbolic" death be accidental: untimely death by other means needs explanations, takes on meanings, hints of pathos or irony or the unselective course of nature.

McCarthy trips over this problem in an unsuccessful story, "The Old Men" (*Cast a Cold Eye*), in which a young man dies what is apparently a "symbolic" death and the reader is left mulling over the unlikely *circumstances* of the death, which distract from the *fact* of the death. An accidental death is convincing and can be passed over quickly and lightly without intruding on the comic tone.

"Killed instantly" is Martha's last, regretful thought. "Luckily," think the Group, Kay's fall was broken by an awning so that "she was not smashed to bits; only her poor neck had been snapped." Of course Kay's death is not funny, but it can't be helped. She is educable; she has taken an honest look at what she is and has determined to stop deceiving herself. She is right in basing her claim to Lakey on the fact that she has nothing to show her. Lakey hated Kay's pretentiousness and ambition, qualities which developed after Lakey's initial attraction to her during their sophomore year. The Kay-That-Never-Was showed off her apartment and her brilliant husband, but the honest Kay has nothing. The Group are mistaken in their judgment that she never grew older and wiser. She learned to live by truth rather than by things.

Not, I hasten to add, that there is anything wrong with *things*, properly applied. Kay would have appreciated the Fortuny dress that Lakey bought her. But she had grown beyond mistaking things for *self*. And among things, besides her apartment and her possessions, we must include not only her husband but ideas that do not work.

The Group is a much better novel than is generally acknowledged. For one thing—and this *is* generally acknowledged—it provides a painless history lesson, being full of the gossip, news, and scandal of the 1930s reliably reported. More important, it explores the tenuous link between ideals and actions. The illusion of progress is always with us, as each generation fancies itself freer and more competent than its parents and adopts whatever is new in the world of ideas as the answer to the old problems it inherits.

The book should not be dismissed as a period piece; it contains the general truths about human nature that we expect in good fiction. What is uniquely successful about *The Group*, however, is McCarthy's use of the narrative voices to show both the unity and the diversity of her characters. Equally remarkable is the art with which she integrates all these materials into a well-built novel. Despite some problems of proportion, the parts of the book cohere, from the ceremonial beginning to the ceremonial conclusion.

6

~·~·~·~·~·~·~·~·~·~·~·~·~·~·~·~·

A Scholarly Maze
and a Question of Justice:
The Groves of Academe

In a broad sense, *The Group* is an academic novel; the central characters never cease to be Vassar girls. Mc-Carthy examines the phenomenon in an essay in *On the Contrary* ("The Vassar Girl"). Eighteen years after her own graduation, she writes that

Vassar had inspired us with the notion that the wide, wide world was our oyster. A few years later, a census was taken, and it was discovered that the average Vassar graduate had two-plus children and was married to a Republican lawyer.

But Vassar attracts girls who expect to be emancipated, made to think for themselves, shaken up. "This dynamic conception of education" accounts for the alumna's being "two persons—the housewife or matron, and the yearner and regretter." Priss is a perfect example. The Group continue to think of themselves in Vassar categories long after graduation. Libby's instinct is to run to Vassar for help when she founders in a difficult Italian book; Dottie's mother reminds her of the example set by her Vassar teachers; Kay goes to the Vassar Club to launch her new life.

The Groves of Academe is an academic novel in the strict sense. Its setting is a progressive college campus in Pennsylvania during the (Senator Joseph) McCarthy era; its characters are college faculty, ad-

ministration, and students. Jocelyn is a fictional college, and if it resembles Bard or Sarah Lawrence or
even Bennington, no matter. It is a little world made
cunningly, complete with a twelve-year history in
which McCarthy satirizes progressive education. Like
New Leeds, it is remote from the larger world, but
it has a foothold in the political climate in which lives
could be ruined by the hint of a Communist affiliation
or even "sympathies." There was Communism in the
past of many Americans whose loyalty was beyond
any just reproach, and McCarthy is one of many writers who condemned the activities of the House Un-
American Activities Committee.

Some of her essays on the subject are printed in
On the Contrary, which also contains "My Confession," an account of McCarthy's left-wing associations
during the thirties. "No News, *or*, What Killed the
Dog" observes that the state of "cultural freedom" in
the country is such that "ideas circulate and the individual is impounded." Although Communist literature is readily available, a person professing Communism is in danger of losing his freedom. "Naming
Names" concludes from the evidence of the Arthur
Miller case that Congress is imposing "the *principle* of
betrayal as a norm of good citizenship."

More directly related to *The Groves of Academe*
is McCarthy's discussion of academic freedom in "The
Contagion of Ideas." Objecting to popular misuse of
the word "right" in a phrase like "the right to teach,"
she points out that teaching is in actuality a *power*
granted by the state and therefore subject to withdrawal by the state. Such a power should not be con-
fused with constitutionally guaranteed *rights*, which
in America are defined as inherent. The danger of
confusing rights with powers is that both alike come
to be regarded as gifts subject to withdrawal at the
pleasure of the state. In *The Groves of Academe*, the

extent of rights, as well as their nature, becomes hopelessly muddled.

According to "The Contagion of Ideas," the educator faces a false dilemma imposed on him by the public, who feel that he must choose between "his traditional notions of freedom and the survival of the free world." In other words, if Communists practice the traditional freedoms, they will destroy freedom for the rest of us. The assumption that Communists can in some subtle way "indoctrinate" innocent youth leads to the conclusion that they must be kept from teaching. It is, McCarthy observes, hard enough to "indoctrinate" students with algebra or punctuation by direct and energetic teaching, let alone with complex ideologies by the indirect means that supposedly transmit communism. But Communists have no *special* right to teach; the question for the liberal college president is not whether to "hire new Communists in order to prove himself a liberal, but whether [to] get rid of the ones he already has on his staff." Since most liberal presidents would not want to fire a teacher for being a Communist, "the usual course is to deny that the teacher concerned is a Communist, thus avoiding the whole question of the 'right to teach,' since this right, openly invoked, will be disputed and the college will probably lose its right, i.e., its power, to harbor him."

It was the patent duty of intellectuals during that era to resist the irrationality of identifying Americans as loyal according to the degree and persistence of their anti-Communism. McCarthy recalls that "most young people who became Communists . . . in the thirties and forties did so either in response to the misery of the depression or in response to the threat of fascism as exemplified by Hitler," but in later years some of these people were stigmatized by that old association. Liberals, in particular academic liberals, were their natural defenders.

But invariably the side of the angels, no matter what the issue, attracts people who weaken rather than strengthen it. Thus, as Ruth Mathewson says, Norine Schmittlapp is not, as she might at first glance appear to be, afflicted by causes; rather, causes are afflicted by Norine.[1] And thus many liberal causes are damaged by the self-serving activism or the "knee-jerk" advocacies of some of their proponents. That is why McCarthy, herself liberal, often criticizes liberals. *The Groves of Academe* is about the consequences of an ill-considered liberal gesture by a college president.

An extremely well structured novel, *The Groves of Academe* moves directly to a conclusion that is stunning yet so consistent with all that has gone before as to seem inevitable. The action takes place within a four-month period, beginning in January with Henry Mulcahy's "amazed, really amazed" reaction to a letter from President Maynard Hoar informing him that he will not be reappointed as literature instructor for the coming academic year and ending with Hoar's announcement to a member of his faculty that he has resigned from his job. The thirteen chapters detail the relentlessly logical sequence of events by which Mulcahy ousts Hoar.

The central character is Mulcahy, but the moral center is Domna Rejnev. At twenty-three, she is the youngest member of Jocelyn's Literature Department. She is intelligent, aristocratic, and scrupulously conscientious; "her very beauty had the quality, not of radiance or softness, but of incorruptibility; it was the beauty of an absolute or a political theorem." She is vulnerable, however, because of her loyalty, and for that reason Mulcahy seeks her out when he is *in extremis*.

She is "conventional," he thinks cynically, "believing in a conventional moral order and shocked by
deviations from it into a sense of helpless guilt toward
the deviator. In other words . . . a true liberal." Mulcahy has no conventional conscience, and he uses
Domna's strengths and weaknesses impartially. He is a
dreadful man. In "Characters in Fiction," McCarthy
explains that her interest in telling his story was "to
know just how it felt to be raging inside the skin of a
Henry Mulcahy." To understand Mulcahy

would get me closer to the mystery, say, of Hitler. . . .
There was no thought of 'tout comprendre, c'est par-
donner.' . . . What I was after was something much more
simple, naïve, and childlike: the satisfaction of the curi-
osity we all feel when we read in the paper of some crime
we cannot imagine committing. . . .

And so we are never far from the consciousness
of this man until the last three chapters, in which we
catch only glimpses of him until we hear Hoar's description of his coup. We are intimate with his
thoughts, we hear his words, we see his fat fingers
and his white freckled face. The story of Jocelyn—a
chapter soberly entitled "Ancient History" and reach-
ing twelve years into the past to the founding of
Jocelyn—is carried by the authorial voice, but most of
what is not in Mulcahy's voice is filtered through the
consciousness of Domna, of Hoar, and more briefly of
other characters. In their obsession with Mulcahy they
echo him, defend, analyze, and interpret him, until at
last Domna decides that they are making too much of
him, that Tolstoy would advise them to "leave it
alone."
When he reads the President's letter, Mulcahy instantly chooses to consider himself fired for political
reasons, and the "transparency" of the move leaves
him "stunned."

> You do not fire a man who has challenged you openly at
> faculty meetings, who has fought . . . for a program of
> salary increases and a lightening of the teaching load, who
> has not feared to point to waste and mismanagement. . . .

In short, Mulcahy has rested his case for a career at
Jocelyn on contentiousness: you do not fire a man
who has opposed you at every turn lest it should seem
that you are firing him *because* he has opposed you.
But Mulcahy has underestimated the President, or, as
he sees it, overestimated him. In any event, he can
"see" now that Hoar is using the dissident Mulcahy "as
a scapegoat to satisfy the reactionary trustees and fund-
raisers." It crosses Mulcahy's mind that he could "ruin
the man forever, at least in liberal circles," by expos-
ing him, an idea that he will put into service at the
novel's end, by which time it is unfortunately true.

Mulcahy came to Jocelyn as a "refugee"; there
were accusations of "Communistic, atheistic tendencies" when he was dimissed from his previous position,
and he has had to disavow Party membership before a
state legislature. Hired by Hoar—"author of a pam-
phlet, 'The Witch Hunt in Our Universities' . . . pho-
togenic, curly-haired evangelist of the right to teach,
leader of torch parades against the loyalty oath, vigorous foe of 'thought control' "—Mulcahy was wel-
comed to Jocelyn as "an exemplar, a modern witness
to the ordeal by slander." Hen, as his friends call him,
has been a trouble-maker during his year and a half at
Jocelyn, inclined to incite tempests in teapots and dis-
inclined to meet classes, keep appointments, maintain
records, and return student papers. He is not, however, being fired. His appointment was a temporary
one intended to tide him over while he sought a more
suitable position.

A prophet of modern literature and a devotee of
James Joyce, Mulcahy carries an ashplant stick in imi-

tation of Stephen Daedalus. He regards himself as a
victim of the "ferocious envy of mediocrity for excel-
lence" in his failure to hold jobs in a "series of
halfway-good colleges." He is remarkably unattrac-
tive, but that too is part of his special destiny.

The unwholesome whiteness of his long, pear-shaped body,
the droop of his trousers, his children's runny noses and
damp bottoms, his wife's woman's complaint, the sand
sprinkling the lashes of his nearsighted, glaucous eyes . . .
were not antipathetic to him but on the contrary lovable,
as a manifesto of ethical difference, like the bleeding holy
pictures of his childhood, the yellowed palms from Palm
Sunday, the vessel of holy water blessed by the Pope.

A symbolist, he is "purposefully" surrounded by objects of a "folkish traditional poverty"—diapers drying on radiators, "nose rags, cleaning rags, lint,
broken toys, potties"—and "all this, in a progressive
community where the casserole and the cocktail and
the disposable diaper reigned . . . had, as he was perfectly aware, a heretical flavor, a pungent breath of
class hatred and contempt."

But Jocelyn is Mulcahy's last chance, and he does
not intend to be fired. His first tentative move toward
resisting the dismissal, confiding in a student, brings
"consolatory visions" of student acitivity on his behalf, visions not to be realized because of the more
effective faculty support engaged. Mulcahy has a student following, however, among the "traditional" students who attend the Saturday night dances. They
admire Cathy as she dances in her wedding dress, enjoying what they see as her triumph over child-rearing
and poverty, and they are gratified by Mulcahy's taking his chaperonage seriously. Other chaperones have
been careless, allowing alcohol and even marijuana to
slip in. These students are apprehensive for Mulcahy—
they hear "rumors of unpaid bills, importunate trades-

men, radiators that had burst from the cold, sickness"
—and they are used to the notice on the door informing then that Dr. Mulcahy will not be able to meet
them today.

Sheila McKay's sympathetic response to his confidence makes Mulcahy recognize the importance of
his wife and children "to any normal onlooker" and
further reminds him that he is always worried about
Catherine's health. "The term, heart murmur, tumbled
at him out of a disordered memory—was it herself or
young Stephen she had been speaking of?"

In order to keep his job, Mulcahy will need the
support of his colleagues. The women probably will
be won to his side by the threat to Cathy's health, but
the men may more readily defend him on grounds of
academic freedom. Mulcahy seeks out Domna as his
first ally and tells her a whole story that will cover
both bases: of the dismissal, of an unwritten promise
that his appointment would be made permanent when
he came to Jocelyn, of Hoar's knowledge of Cathy's
grave condition and therefore his culpability in
jeopardizing her life by firing Mulcahy, and, finally
and carefully, of his membership in the Communist
Party as "one of those unfortunate prisoners" of the
Party, persecuted alike by Communists, who know
that he is their enemy, and by anti-Communists, who
do not know that. Hoar has, Mulcahy tells Domna,
obviously found out about the old affiliation and is
firing him for it. "That he had never, as it happened,
chanced to join the Communist Party organizationally
did not diminish the truth of this revelation," he reflects. Here is the irony at the center of the book.
Mulcahy prides himself on being the first, "so far as he
knew, in all history, to expose the existence of a frame-
up by framing himself first." Surely a liberal president
will retain a Communist.

At the instigation of Domna, members of the Lit-

erature Department convene to draft a petition in
support of Mulcahy. By traditional standards, Mulcahy has the best credentials on the literature faculty.
He has its only Ph.D. and is the only member whose
publications have won recognition outside of Jocelyn.
Jocelyn is, however, not a traditional college, and ad-
vanced degrees and publications are not requirements
imposed on the faculty. Mulcahy's colleagues are also
impressed by his intelligence, by the "preternatural
activity" of his brain, but he is without other redeem-
ing qualities.

Furness, a cynic who does not trust Mulcahy anyway, refuses to participate in the effort to have him
retained. Partly because he is department chairman, he
is all too aware of Mulcahy's shortcomings, and he
insists that if the man is to be made the object of
charity, his defenders should plead frankly on the basis
of his need for the job. "Why bring in all this stuff
about Cathy and Hen's being a prisoner of the Party,
if you really think it's a straight case of merit going
unrewarded?"

Domna, although deeply concerned for Cathy, insists that nonethless, Mulcahy is both competent and
brilliant and that, other things being equal, a particular
effort should be made on behalf of anyone in his unfortunate circumstances. The like-minded Alma Fortune, forty, widowed and spinsterish, counsels avoiding the appearance of evil; even if it is not, Mulcahy's
dismissal might seem to be political. But foreseeing
the outcome of the discussion, she has already written
her letter of resignation. John Bentkoop supports
Mulcahy on the grounds that the college needs a theist. Van Tour, who "like many teachers of English . . .
was not able to think very clearly," earnestly worries
the question of academic freedom. And Aristide
Poncy tries to be judicious as a nonvoting emissary

from the French Department. They are academic types brought roundly to life, endlessly talking; they talk their way to a stalemate, for unanimity is essential and Furness will not join them. There will be no petition.

The case is won by a delegation of two. Domna and Bentkoop go to the President, who is impressed by their integrity and by this demonstration of faculty respect for Mulcahy's abilities; the Communist affiliation is not even brought up. Domna has dinner the same night with the Mulcahys, and Cathy, after having too much to drink, lets it slip that she has known all along about the struggle for her husband's job. Since Mulcahy has assured Domna that this information could be fatal to Cathy and had to be kept from her at any cost, Domna is shocked by the revelation and flees the Mulcahys as soon as she gracefully can.

The renewal of Mulcahy's contract coincides therefore with his estrangement from the chief engineer of his salvation. Far from being contrite for his deception, he is angered by Domna's "betrayal" of him and wonders whether she has "gone a little mad, as people will, when they find that they have been seen in their true colors"—in this case, unwilling to accept cheerfully the news that friendship has been exploited. Mulcahy makes a new friend in the department, Ellison, always noticeably absent from the meetings about Mulcahy; he has now determined the wind's direction and is ready to set sail with Mulcahy. Jocelyn is excited about a poetry conference slated for April, and Ellison and Mulcahy set about undercutting Domna's standing in the department by scheming to exclude her from the planning of the symposium.

When Domna and Alma hear rumors that Mulcahy is plotting to sabotage the symposium, they are alarmed at the possibility that the college will be dis-

graced. They are now acutely aware of Mulcahy's failings, which they did not notice before urging his re-
tention, and their responsiblity in the matter has
begun to bother them. Thus they report the rumors to
Furness, who is always ready to believe the worst, and
once again Mulcahy is the center of departmental agitation. When Furness confronts Mulcahy, Ellison in-
tervenes to say that he has inspired some of the rumors
in order to excite interest in the symposium.

Despite apprehensions, the conference comes off
reasonably well, but it provides another crisis. Among
the visiting poets is a former Party member, the "poet
of the masses." Keogh hails an evasive Mulcahy during
one gathering, reminding him of old acquaintance. "I
was using my Party name, then." Overhearing, Furness and Hoar are dumbfounded. They were certain
that Mulcahy was never a Communist. If he was, Hoar
thinks, "I'll have the trustees on my back again. . . .
Poor devil, poor hunted devil . . . he *was* perjured,
apparently, before the state legislature."

The "terrible" thought strikes that Mulcahy may
still be a Communist. "We've got to cover this thing
up, as soon as we can find out what to cover," Hoar
cries to Furness, and so it happens that the poet of the
masses is "shaken awake" early in the morning and
taken, "dazed, breakfastless, and bleeding from a quick
shave" to the President's office, where Hoar, Furness,
Domna, and Bentkoop wait to hear, at last, the truth.
Keogh is able to tell them authoritatively that Mulcahy never joined the Party. Afterward, wondering if
even by exonerating Mulcahy he has somehow played
the "stool-pigeon," Keogh tells Mulcahy about the interview in order to undo any harm that he may have
done.

Albeit innocently, he thereby provides Mulcahy
with the ultimate weapon. In a "shocking scene," a

"shattering experience" which Hoar describes to
Bentkoop over the telephone, Mulcahy

literally shook his fist in Maynard's face, threatened to
expose him to the A.A.U.P., and to every liberal magazine
and newspaper in the country. He was going to write a
sequel to the President's magazine article that would reveal to the whole world the true story of a professional
liberal: a story of personal molestation, spying, surveillance,
corruption of students by faculty stool-pigeons.

Hoar has resigned. No matter how "twisted," what
Mulcahy says is true "on the surface." "I saw that I
was too much incriminated. The college would never
get rid of him as long as I was at the tiller." The novel
ends with Hoar's "noble voice" declaiming from Cicero's oration, "How far at length, O Catiline, will
you abuse our patience?"
    What Mulcahy wants, he tells Hoar, is "justice.
Justice for myself as a superior individual and for my
family." He claims his rights: "the right to pursue his
profession, the right to teach without interference or
meddling, the right to bring up his family in reasonable
circumstances." Ordinary justice relates to fact, but
with Mulcahy "justice" in whatever achieves his
"rights," which are defined solely by his will.
    His identification with Joyce is part of a "delu-
sional system" in which, Domna tells Bentkoop,
"Henry Mulcahy is Christ in the disguise of Bloom
and Earwicker, the family man, the fathers eternal and
consubstantial with the son." Bentkoop adds that
Christ's experience patterns classical paranoia, shown
by a "belief in divine origin, special calling . . . the cult
of exclusive disciples, betrayal, justification." The
words that come to Mulcahy's mind express the con-
stancy and depth of his self-reverence: *"Ite missa est,"*
he tells Domna of his career at Jocelyn; Hoar's hands
are as "clean as Pilate's," he thinks. While he licks his

little wooden spoon, his ice cream melts in a paper-and-plastic "chalice." Friends who have any reservations "betray" or "lose faith in" him, which is "apostasy." He requires absolute loyalty and uncritical devotion.

Mulcahy is without humor. He was quite serious about the twenty thousand eggs when he challenged the dietitian to "unscramble" their history. Upon Domna's laughing admission that she and some others felt that he went a little far on that occasion, Mulcahy grimly reflects that she has "betrayed" him. Even his pun is no occasion for levity; such word play links him with Shakespeare and Joyce, "our two greatest writers." He resents Furness's "jocular allusions" to his alleged Party membership because "it stung him to see that Furness had so little appreciation of his life. . . . To be told that we would be ludicrous in any life-role, even an uncongenial one, is an insult to our sense of human possibility."

Nothing by way of service is ever enough. Informed that Domna and Alma have thought of resigning if he is turned down, Mulcahy inquires "wistfully," "Just you and Alma?" Alma's resignation on his behalf, once it is a *fait accompli*, strikes him as "intrinsically selfish." When his contract is renewed, he immediately begins a probe of faculty reaction to his complaint that his salary is inadequate, but he finds opinion "neutral." The "common prescription" that he try writing for money is the "final insult to his talent and to a lifetime of sacrifice to an anti-commercial ideal."

Mulcahy is a baleful influence. At the crucial dinner, Cathy tells Domna that one person loves another's "essence," not the "dross of appearance"; but essence notwithstanding, Domna holds no brief for liars. In an all-night postmortem with the Bentkoops, she confesses that she lied to Hoar: "My students do not praise Henry." At the time, she told the President what she believed to be true—that students admired

Henry—but she abandoned "exactitude" and invented evidence to support her statement. In seeking the essence of justice for her friend, she abused literal truth in a way that she would not have done for herself. Domna exists in a world of facts in which it is possible, and dishonorable, to lie.

Mulcahy, on the other hand, is incapable of dishonesty. He "looks at truth with the eyes of a literary critic," Bentkoop explains, "and measures a statement by its persuasiveness. If he himself can be persuaded he accepts the moot statement as established. . . . 'Is it true?' you want to know, but the question's irrelevant and footless." Bentkoop, who considers the department too exclusively formalistic in its approach to literature, considers Mulcahy valuable for his emphasis on ideas, on universals and first principles: students "take to them like catnip." The opinion gains credibility on the evidence of Mulcahy's small but devoted band of exploited student followers. Although Mulcahy may be of the devil's party, Bentkoop philosophically grants that "the devil is a theist, too." It is an interesting argument which imbues Bentkoop's advocacy of Mulcahy with a validity lacking in Domna's. She is a formalist and an atheist. After this conversation, however, she looks to Tolstoy, her favorite writer, for an answer, and she finds it; but it is too late to "leave it alone."

Domna did not like Henry when she first met him, and she has continued to be physically repelled by him, as he knows. Pleading his case at the faculty meeting, she urged the principle of *noblesse oblige*. After the discovery of his moral baseness, she restores the class barrier; "one has only to look at Henry to imagine the matrix that formed him—a poor heredity, hagiolatrous parents, a nasty and narrow environment, sweets, eyestrain, dental caries." In her friendship with Mulcahy, Domna has been liberal—that is, democratic

—but the overcoming of repugnance is not in itself an authentic end.

Neither is the hiring of a dissident. Maynard Hoar is an attractive character, flexible, intelligent, and compassionate; but one cannot escape the implications of his name or of McCarthy's description.

Like all such official types, he specialized in being his own antithesis; strong but understanding, boisterous but grave, pragmatic but speculative. . . . The necessity of encompassing such opposites had left him with a little wobble of uncertainty in the center of his personality. . . .

Although once "quite a classicist," Hoar presides over a school in which students, according to the intentions of the founder, "were simply to be free, spontaneous, and coeducational." He was hopeful of measuring student potential and "directing it into the proper channels for maximum self-realization"; this was to be done in the nonjudgmental manner of the scientific experiment.

If the student failed to go in the direction indicated by the results of his testing, or in any direction at all, this was noted down and in time communicated to his parents, merely as a matter of interest—to push him in any way would be a violation of the neutrality of the experiment.

Unfortunately and not surprisingly, the approach did not work.

Its two surviving practices are periodically scrutinized, found wanting, and preserved. The first, the field-period—four weeks in February when the students are sent forth to learn through *doing*—survives because of the faculty plurality which every year "shamelessly" vote to "save their precious vacation." The second, individual instruction, which works well enough when there is laboratory or studio work to be supervised, imposes a strenuous hardship on teachers in the humanities, who cannot manage the voluminous reading required for detailed discussions of numerous individual projects. Thus students often find themselves pursuing not their own interests— often vague, in any case—but those of their instructors, who might as well double up in the tutorial and abandon the claim to individual instruction.

Any such suggestion is always sternly vetoed by the President. "Only individual instruction could justify the high tuition, which alone kept the college going," and President Hoar "not only believed with all his heart in the merits of individual instruction but knew this belief to be necessary to his own and the college's survival."

Hoar's motives are adulterated. He tries to be both honorable and practical, an aim which can strain the truth. He does believe in individual instruction, and it would be unkind to assume that the motive of survival outweighs the motive of conviction. But the "little wobble" is his undoing. He appointed Mulcahy because of his unfortunate history, not in spite of it; there was no job open at Jocelyn. His doing so was a humane act, but it also enhanced his reputation as a liberal and provided him with material for another article at the expense of the college. When he has opportunity and cause to "rid" Jocelyn of this person, he wobbles in the direction of Mulcahy's defenders, who report that students praise him. Even if this were true, it would hardly be sufficient answer to the arguments against Mulcahy, who disapproves of the methods at Jocelyn, whose professional abilities fill no needs at Jocelyn, and who is troublesome and unreliable.

Mulcahy is unemployable; that is his strength, the sole reason he remains employed. Hired as a martyr and retained as an object of charity, he prevails. He cannot be dismissed for cause any more than he could

have been hired for cause. All those who are involved
with him are too decent to want him to suffer justice
based on facts.

The arrival of the poets provides a welcome relief
from the malevolent centrality of Mulcahy. He is seen
from time to time—fetching poets in his old Plymouth,
darting to the podium with a message, replying "mis-
trustfully" to Keogh's greeting—but his chief interest
in the symposium lies in the small power play during
the planning. The rest of the faculty anxiously manage
logistics, transportation, and timing, and the poets are
mildly unmanageable from the time when they ignore
the recommended train and straggle in one by one.

One deaf old poet appeared in the morning and spent the
whole day wandering about the campus, lonely as a cloud.
One, taking unfair advantage of the provision for expenses,
arrived by plane in Pittsburgh, whence he telephoned collect. . . . The poet of the masses hitchhiked. . . . Only one,
a woman lyricist, arrived at the proper time and place, and
this, as it turned out, proved most inconvenient.

Bearing resemblances to poets living and dead,
they are individualized by epithets as an old poet or
the whiskered poet, or grouped as the younger poets
and the older poets, and two or three are actually
named. But most often they are referred to generically
in numbers to be rounded up or transported by car-
fuls. Jocelyn is a bit awed by the responsibility of
caring for poets. The poets, however, are quite accustomed to conferences of this sort, and they take the
worldly view that the affair is a "mutual exploitation"
which, if they can avoid the faculty, will provide
them with a chance to drink and talk with their
friends.

They are naturally a bit testy when only sherry is
served at the first gathering, they are rudely surprised
at the "tactful literacy" of Alma's introduction, and

they are irritated when the rules of etiquette toward poets are violated. Van Tour in his morning session has the "idiocy" to call on the publishers' representatives for a few words on modern poetry, and the small informal audience is treated to the observation that modern poetry does not communicate. The poets politely refrain from disavowing any desire to communicate with "these persons," whom they could hardly reach anyway since the persons in question do not read poetry; but when Van Tour lets the discussion follow the inevitable course to a student's challenge to have a poet explicate his own poem, he earns the scorn of the "choleric" poet.

There is, as a matter of fact, precious little communication of any kind at the conference. The students are baffled by the talks, and the poets miss the point of the questions. For Hoar, things are off to a bad start when Miss Mansell is late to dinner and the first session has to begin late. This "lady poet" turns her body "slowly from the waist" toward people who address her, due to a "trick of her corseting," a habit which makes Hoar feel like "something infinitely small, at the other end of a telescope."

Having anticipated a Platonic "banquet of the mind," Hoar is further discomfited to hear, from the assembled poets, "a clamor of personal allusions . . . a good deal of profanity from the younger members, and several unflattering references to members of his own faculty."

Miss Mansell's opening lecture is disconcerting in a different way. Her subject is Virgil. The students suppose that the Mantuan is a modern poet as yet unknown to their faculty; only a few scholarship students who have not had the "good fortune to be progressively educated" have heard of him, and they emit "stifled cries of 'Let me out of here' and 'This is where I came in.'" The "passion and tragic nobility" of her

Dido is a "rare treat" to Hoar, but he knows that he will pay "at the bench of progressive judgment" for a supposed "connivance in this reactionary coup of the Literature department." One member of Social Sciences calls out to Hoar, "Fine stuff," but being a history teacher, he has the occupational weakness of a "tolerance for the past."

When the second poet, "pinkly smiling," announces that he will speak on Lucretius, the faculty wonder whether the poets are making fun of the students. They recall that this poet inquired whether Jocelyn was the "fabled college where everything is run backward" and received with "an air of gentle disappointment" the answer that "no, indeed, it was not, that the courses ran normally from the immediate past to the present." No guile is apparent in the talk, it turns out, but there is "nothing new" in it, and it is so lucid "that the best disposal that the Literature faculty could make of it was to assume that they had not understood it."

After the lecture, the poet of the masses presents an unscheduled recitation of the old poet's poems, to the delight of the audience, save the other poets. Furness, attending Hoar as a kind of guide through this intellectual underworld, explains that true poets honor the "natural antagonism" between poet and reader and that by this performance Keogh has shown himself to be "not really a poet." Poets flock to conferences on the Contemporary Neglect of Poetry to be assured that they are not loved. Keogh is temporarily ostracized by the other poets; Hoar is shocked to see him standing alone and, out of hospitality, is moving toward him when Keogh greets Mulcahy.

As for Keogh, he is determinedly a spectator, a poet of the road, a free spirit, a middle-aged youth, not much of a poet at all. To Jocelyn's students an interesting relic of a remote and irrelevant past (the thirties), to the other poets, when they relent, he is "unobjectionable" as a man of action. Untamed, he is wary of the summons to Hoar's office, and hostile, but he reminds himself that these people are human beings. Questioning the earthy and blunt Keogh, Hoar sounds unctuous and insincere: "We have no idea of using this information in any way, shape, or form. We are all liberals . . . shocked and sickened by the reign of terror in our colleges." Like a cautious animal, Keogh sits "absolutely still" listening and then accepts Hoar's pamphlets as evidence of good faith. (He will toss them, unread, into a trash bin when he is out of sight.) Having cleared Mulcahy of the charge of Communism, Keogh fears that he has been "taken in," but after making amends by telling Mulcahy what he has done, he sees Domna on campus and wonders:

Did he owe it to her to tell her what he had just told this shit, Mulcahy, etc., etc.? But as the ridiculous question, like a repeating decimal, propounded itself to him, he struck his open left hand a blow with his right fist. No, he inwardly shouted to himself; *Keogh, keep out of this or they will get you.*

Escape from the "academic maze" costs Maynard Hoar a high price. Blackmailed by the outraged, outrageous Mulcahy, Hoar actually considers bribing the man to leave Jocelyn; he also thinks of Samson—bringing the temple down. But he chooses the more moderate course of resignation, a gesture that he tells Bentkoop is, in a way, his farewell to progressivism. When he was young, he wanted to be a lawyer and his hero was Cicero. He has experienced a kind of epiphany during the symposium, through the classical content of the lectures so alien to Jocelyn students awash in the unformed present, through his astonishment at the sight of *nuns* on the Jocelyn campus: "I thought I had gone mad."

Nuns are traditional, continuous with the past, emblematic of discipline, community, and service. Only a page or two earlier, Furness has been telling the taciturn poets (who feel that he is preempting their right to make such observations) that the "progressive methodology . . . with its emphasis on faith and individual salvation, is a Protestant return to the Old Testament." Furness genuinely likes the modern as "subversive" of the past. But Hoar, like the young Mary of *Memories of a Catholic Girlhood*, is attuned to the rule of law under which facts relate to truth and both relate to justice. Like her, he loses sympathy with the rebel Catiline.

Lest we reach any facile conclusions about the novel's endorsement of the traditional over the progressive, it is well to point out that everybody thinks the villainous Mulcahy is equipped to do well in a traditional college. It is not because of Jocelyn's progressive methods, either, that so much of what goes on in faculty meetings is sophisticated niggling or that student uprisings threaten over Lilliputian issues (whether plates in the dining hall should be passed clockwise or counterclockwise). The homely details of small-college life everywhere are magnified by the microscope through which Jocelyn is viewed: the waste of energy on trivia, the all-too-human motives often underlying the high rhetoric and sharp wit, the endless agonizing over minute questions, the jealousy with which intellectual territories are guarded and better students coveted. As for the end result, the old-timers among the teachers know that the student body has always a "large percentage of trouble-makers and a handful of gifted creatures who would redeem the whole." It is the theory rather than the practice of progressive education that comes under attack.

The Groves of Academe is probably McCarthy's best novel, perhaps the best academic novel American literature has produced. Its satire is amiable, the "norm" of right reason and morality clearly implied, the dilemma—what to do about a man like Mulcahy—acknowledged as a true, not a false, dilemma. The characters are well realized, save Bentkoop, who, being a realist and a theist, is a little hard to pin down. Ideas, which are the very fabric of the novel, are the properties of the characters; one rarely feels that a character is conjured up to serve merely as a mouthpiece. The essence and voice of Mulcahy are so perfectly rendered that, repelled as we are, we nonetheless respond to him in human terms, are swept along by his arguments—for he *is* intelligent—or are moved to pity—for he *does* need his job. Finally, *The Groves of Academe* is an extremely well made novel, with all its parts relevant to the advancement of its simple but exquisite plot.

7

The Liberal Imagination
and the Modern Dilemma:
Birds of America

Birds of America is the story of the coming of age of
Peter Levi. A young liberal idealist, Peter is the son of
Rosamund Brown of Ohio and her first husband, an
anti-Fascist Italian Jew who emigrated to the United
States during World War II. Peter is a patriot whose
political milieu is shaped by the civil rights movement
and the early stages of the war in Vietnam.

Peter has the strong moral sense that is characteristic of McCarthy's heroines, but he is shy and lacks
their pleasure in being different and their desire to
shock; and he measures the significance of his actions
against the needs of mankind rather than the special
requirements of a small society. An egalitarian, Peter
attempts to order his life around Kantian ethics, holding as his touchstones two maxims in particular: "The
Other is always an End" and "Behave as if thy maxim
could be a universal law."

The story is told entirely from Peter's point of
view, but the use of his voice imposes no stringent
limitations on McCarthy's style; he is educated, articulate, and observant. He uses slang and clichés with the
license of the college student but not to the point of
sacrificing literacy. The style is full of allusions appropriate to the college junior that he is: Peter tacks
from Scylla to Charybdis, he sinks into the arms of
Morpheus, he wonders whether a friend is doing a

Sydney Carton. A serious young man, he can nonetheless see the ridiculous in himself as in others: He hears himself caw like the Raven; he knows that to a policeman he is a weedy member of the draft pool; he is Peter Levi, famed linguist, when his French fails him. Occasionally he falls into the attitude of the supercilious youth, but not for long. He is often argumentative —not contentious—because he loves to work things out logically. When he becomes irritated, he quickly repents, and compassion or his peaceable nature overrides the irritation.

Although the voice is convincing and the character consistent and likable, the book is seriously flawed. It is about Peter's developing mind, but nonetheless his fresh discoveries of old ideas grow tedious, no matter how much we sympathize. Rosamund's menus and traditions are thematically important, but the lists and catalogues numb the mind. And we wonder whether we must know so much about Paris toilets in order to understand that Peter is disgusted and baffled by the copious droppings so unnaturally left exposed and reeking.

The novel is put together carefully. The action begins during the summer of 1964 and runs to Valentine's Day, 1965; it is set in Rocky Port, Maine, in Paris, and in Rome. The first and last scenes depend upon birds, an owl and a swan; but the birds of the title are of the human as well as the feathered sort, and both kinds provide a unifying motif. Comparison also ties the materials together. Thanksgiving Day in Paris recalls a Thanksgiving four years earlier in Rocky Port, and both are "traditional," or perhaps neither is. Past and present, two Christmas parties, two encounters with policemen, Paris and Rome, even Rome and Rocky Port are set against each other explicitly or implicitly, and the similarities and contrasts help develop the interrelated themes of nature, art, tradition,

and morality. Peter's mentor, Kant, is present at the
beginning through his maxims, at the end in Peter's
hallucination. Yet in spite of all of these structural
aids, the novel fails as a whole. Once Peter leaves
Rocky Port, his story becomes a kind of pilgrim's progress, an intellectual biography in which people and
events provide him chiefly with food for thought.

The Rocky Port section—which appeared, in
slightly different form, in the *Southern Review*, 1965—
is the best. Almost certainly fictionalizing her relationship with her own son, McCarthy puts a good deal of
herself into Rosamund Brown, celebrated harpsichord-
ist and mother of Peter. The sophisticated Peter was
quite aware of his Oedipal phase as he lived it. At
fifteen, he realized a dream of long standing when
Rosamund was in the "trial separation" stage of her
second marriage (she has since then married for the
third time) and he and she went to live by themselves
in Rocky Port during the fall and winter months. The
novel begins four years later, when they are back in
Rocky Port for the summer before Peter goes to the
Sorbonne for his junior year.

Peter is a nature lover. In general McCarthy has
rather ignored nature, and so have her characters.
Even in portraying New Leeds, a seaside village, she
does little with the natural setting. Rocky Port is
something like New Leeds, perhaps a decade later, but
where New Leeds is comically exaggerated, Rocky
Port is grimly exposed. In an outbreak of progress
aggravated by bad taste, the Rocky Port species has
spoiled its legacies of nature and tradition and reduced
the little village to a characterless tourist town. "You
have to expect changes," Peter is told by various residents, including the woman who informs him, in the
opening scene, that the great horned owl is dead. Peter
has gone to the sanctuary to visit his old friend, never
having thought that like "any senior citizen," the

caged bird could just "pass away." He is grieved by
the loss. He misses, too, three cormorants that he used
to watch from his window.

Rocky Port is now connected to New York by
regular air service and by a new highway, facilities
which render it easily accessible to people who identify themselves as escapees from the rat race. Though
politically liberal, Peter is a traditionalist: "Except in
the field of civil rights, he was opposed to progress in
any direction, including backward, which was the direction Rocky Port seemed to be heading in." Rustic
signs have replaced the old "commercial" ones, and
houses have "sprouted little historical notices." Over
the landlady's protest, Rosamund has removed one
identifying her house as a former ship's chandler's
home and shop.

The artful historicity is a gratuitous addition to
Rocky Port, but more distressing are the subtractions.
Besides the birds, Peter misses a waterfall which
has vanished in some way probably connected with
highway construction. And he and Rosamund are
constantly thwarted in their efforts to assemble the
merchandise necessary for her game of preparing authentic American meals. Such items as bean pots were
always hard to get in Rocky Port, but now even
muffin tins are disappearing from the shops, along with
buttons and other homely items. The local fish market
offers convenience foods. "Am I wrong," demands
Rosamund, "to want a whole fresh fish—with head
and bones—on the seashore?" The butcher has no
hens. "Folks here don't make soup like they used to.
Guess we're kind of spoiled." More optimistic than
Rosamund in interpreting the signs of the time, Peter
suggests, "Maybe *you're* spoiled, Mother. Only a few
rich people with cooks can afford the kind of food
you like."

Nonetheless, Rocky Port is committed to "tradition," and it annually commemorates the Battle of Rocky Port with a two-day "jamboree." Rosamund's eager offer to make baked beans and ice cream for the fair on the village green is firmly refused because the company which sells colas and hot dogs also handles ice cream. Mrs. Curtis recalls the old days when "people rushed around . . . to get that one's chicken pie or that one's lobster salad," but observes that the commercial outfits save "a lot of trouble." Only the cakes for the cake sale are still made from scratch. Peter and his mother console themselves by looking forward to the parade, the tours of old houses and gardens, and the flower-arranging contests.

But the whole celebration is a disaster. The neglected "gardens" are all but flowerless; the houses are "tacky"; the "flower" arrangements are weedy and the contest is spoiled by the revelation that the winners in one division cheated by buying their materials from a florist. On the second morning, the police demand restoration of the historical notice to Rosamund's house; after a small fracas, Peter and his mother are locked up in the Rocky Port jail. Peter anticipated incarceration this summer before his parents vetoed his plan to go to Mississippi with the Students for Civil Rights; "you went there knowing you might be arrested." But this adventure, unexpected and pointless, is different. "One minute he was peacefully watering the geraniums and the next he was aiming a feeble left at a policeman's jaw."

Another difference, Peter's friend the admiral explains, is that Rocky Port police are less well acquainted with the fine points of law than their Mississippi counterparts, who have to know the law to "use it against you." He advises Peter not to insist on technicalities. The affair will blow over, and Rosamund can send the judge and the chief of police one of her albums. Peter's sense of justice is offended at this use of his mother's position.

They *ought* to stand trial, he considered. The charges were true. And what was their defense? That a policeman had called him "Buster" and had asked for his draft card. . . . If there was any justice in Rocky Port, they should be lucky to get off with a suspended sentence.

He opposes "cops' throwing their weight around," but they do, and the consequences should follow impartially.

The jail porch is the ideal vantage point for watching the fireworks display. When the jailer leads him there, Peter finds Rosamund comfortably smoking a cigarette with the waitress who doubles as matron. It is the most pleasant event of the entire fair.

Peter crosses the Atlantic by ship in order to take his motorbike with him, planning a leisurely overland trip to Paris before checking in at the Sorbonne. After mangling a French phrase at Le Havre, however, he loses control to the extent that he winds up unhappily traveling to Paris by train in the company of three aging American schoolteachers. Peter hopes that he and his fellow students will help to improve French impressions of Americans; anti-Americanism troubles him partly because he feels it, too, in light of the "assorted atrocities" committed in the United States by racists.

But the first compatriots he meets on French soil, though distinctly prejudiced, are more embarrassing than sinister. Learning that his father is Italian, the teachers assume that his mother is too, and they inquire whether she makes "the real spaghetti" and "those pizza pies," which the cosmopolitan Peter knows do not constitute "the real" Italian cuisine; but there is too much here to answer in brief, and Peter

dodges by informing the women that his mother has
had "a jag of cooking American," whereupon they approve of her giving him the same as his friends had,
"in *their homes*." After they have registered several
such misapprehensions, Peter seizes an opportunity to
get one truth on the record by informing the women
that his father is a Jew, a heritage which they deli-
cately patronize: "to us you're a fellow-American, regardless of creed or color." They mean well, however,
and Peter is touched by their attempts to be helpful to
a youthful traveler.

At the depot in Paris, he is eager to escape them;
he told the truth when he petulantly denied being the
young man they had seen with a motorcycle, but now
he needs to claim his motor*bike* without their seeing
him. When they appear, still helpful, Peter glimpses a
salesman whom he met on the ship and in desperation
hails him as an old friend. Kindly, the man sweeps him
away to a military hotel, where Peter spends his first
night in Paris passing for a general's wife's nephew.

There follows a twenty-eight-page letter from
Peter to his mother. He finally has his own apartment.
Living in a series of hotels put his principles to a test
which devolved upon the question of tipping the cham-
bermaids; if he tipped, he got better service. In one
hotel, the maid rushed ahead of him to the communal
toilet to clean it. "If the other inhabitants had to use a
dirty, stinking toilet, why should I be the exception?
In fact, it was her job to clean the toilet." Kant was no
help. If nobody tipped, it would be hard on the cham-
bermaids; if everybody did, it would be hard on people who could not afford to. The letter is given to
such reflections, discussing, for example, the relationship of aesthetics to ethics and charging Rosamund
with confusing the two—aesthetics is not a proper
guide to conduct because it is undemocratic. In the
city of the French Revolution, Peter decides that

equality is an idea which has never been tried; he would like to see it tested to find out whether it works.

He comes back, before closing, to the communal toilets. Unable to take minimal use of them and depart, he scrubbed them and left them gleaming. "And I couldn't help feeling moral about it—judging my predecessors in the toilet in a highly unfavorable way. . . . But if I really believed in equality, why was I glad to be the exception?"

Save for a Norwegian student who has been deported and an Italian revolutionary, the friends Peter makes in Paris are Americans; the only congenial French people he meets are members of the bird-watching group he joins. Once, while taking his plant for a walk, he witnesses a confrontation between student demonstrators and police; as the police swing their "pretty blue capes," he approves of their graceful handling of the affair until he realizes that the capes are lined with lead. Having just made the acquaintance of a young Polish American, Peter sees him arrested and knows him to be innocent. Pursuing justice for his new friend, Peter narrowly escapes being hit by the paddy wagon; as he leaps out of the way, he sends his plant flying to decapitation in the city of the guillotine. Feeling responsible for Makowski, Peter makes a nuisance of himself with a bureaucrat in the consulate at the American Embassy until he establishes that the young man has been released.

Peter celebrates Thanksgiving with an American general and his wife. The nicest feature of the dinner party, in Peter's opinion, is a girl named Roberta Scott, a medical student and vegetarian; he watches, fascinated, her intricate maneuvers to separate vegetable morsels from the contaminating turkey and gravy that the general has heaped on her plate with sadistic hospitality. While admiring her integrity, Peter feels that she is rather spoiling things for the rest of them,

who cannot stop questioning her and urging her to
eat. When the subject finally turns to the war in Vietnam, it looks as if Peter and the general are on the
same side, for the general favors America's winding up
its business there. Asked about the political difficulty
of pulling out, however, he explodes: "For Christ's
sake, I said 'wind it up.' " This, he feels, can be ac-
complished by bombing Hanoi. Horrified, Peter joins
the argument for a time and then resorts to verbal
assault: "You don't give a damn about your country,
you stupid patriot." But he is by now drunk enough to
be forgiven, and his hostess kindly nurses him until he is
sufficiently recovered to participate in the final activity of the American holiday, a softball game.

Peter is elated to receive an invitation to a Christmas party. Although it comes from strangers, it is issued "at the kind suggestion of Miss Roberta Scott,"
but incredibly, Roberta is not at the party. She is away
from Paris with her *petit ami*, a doctor who is separated from his wife. "Stupefied" by this bit of news,
Peter complains to his friend Sylvanus (Silly) Platt:
"You assume that if somebody's a puritan, they're a
puritan all the way. . . . You'd think you had the right
to assume that." Silly is sympathetic, even though he
himself is a somewhat decadent youth. He wears his
brother's Phi Beta Kappa key and is pleased to have an
odd name that opens conversations; with various such
"ploys," he works on getting invited into French
"homes" and into the lives of wealthy older women.

In Rome during Christmas vacation Peter takes in
as much as he can of frescoes, sculptures, and build-
ings. He runs into his adviser from the Sorbonne and
is interested and amused to learn that Mr. Small is
studying tourism, a project financed by educational
grants and carried out by being a tourist. Having
found that the crush of his fellow tourists does a lot to
spoil things for him, Peter has bought a pair of ear-

plugs to shut out their voices, but Mr. Small depre-
cates "those snobs who distinguish between class tourism and mass tourism." Mr. Small, however, is a chiseler
and a Philistine, and he tries to cheat Peter on their
luncheon tab.

Back in Paris, where poverty seems worse than in
the warmer climate of Rome, Peter is increasingly
pained by the *clochards*, the drunks who sleep on the
streets. His concierge relishes telling Peter about her
battle to prevent their sleeping in the hallways of her
building, and he can see her point: the one who left
cigarette butts in the elevator one night could easily
have reduced the entire building to ashes. When he
finds a drunk woman on his stairway one night, he can
morally neither leave her there to imperil the "fire-
trap" that he lives in nor put her out in the cold. He
can see nothing to do but take her to his room, give
her a chance to clean herself up, feed her, and treat
her as a fellow creature. But the woman does not clean
herself; she eats only when bribed with wine; and she
is clearly no happier to be there than Peter is to have
her. In the morning, she is gone, there is urine on the
floor, and Peter's doorknob is missing.

There is bad news in the morning papers; the
United States has begun bombing North Vietnam.
Peter and Silly go to the zoo to distract themselves.
Silly likes animals, but he enjoys playing games that to
Peter seem cruel and dangerous. When he teases the
swans by tossing peanuts between them until they
grow quarrelsome, Peter offers, in a "countermove,"
to feed the black swan from his hand, and the bird
attacks him.

Blood poisoning lands Peter in the hospital, and a
reaction to penicillin nearly kills him. When he re-
gains lucidity on Valentine's Day, his mother is with
him. She is on her way to Poland on a tour for the
State Department. But Peter has had other visitors in

his delirium. Chief among them was Kant, come to tell him a sad truth: "Perhaps you have guessed it. Nature is dead, *mein kind*."

Peter at first understands him to say that God is dead, an old piece of news and not so tragic; Peter has always lived without God. Nature's death is another matter, for he has always depended upon Nature, honoring her moral laws. At fifteen, he was romantic: "his love for his mother coincided with his love of Nature and of the austere New England landscape." He liked to imagine that he and his mother, discovering hidden features like the owl, were pioneers in the wilderness. When he was generous with Rosamund, his other mother rewarded him, he thought, with the wonderful spectacle of apple blossoms at Thanksgiving. When he forgot about Nature, he was punished; his father, "like black retribution," spirited him away to boarding school and the idyl was over. But when he is nineteen, he realizes that he followed inclination, not duty, in those pre-Kantian days, equating happiness with virtue.

Actually, visiting the owl had begun to bother Peter even then. He wanted to feed the bird but feared that it would be unable to fend for itself after its long captivity or would wreak havoc among the smaller creatures in the sanctuary. Four years later, finding the "lonely hooter" missing, Peter is grief-stricken; but he also knows that he must *do* something, i.e., overcome his shyness and inquire of the owl's nearest neighbor what has become of the bird. Otherwise, "it would be as if he did not care," a sin against Nature. Peter not only loves but feels responsible for Nature.

His duty to Nature includes the plant world. He likes the idea that "mortal man was put into the world to be the husbandman of immortal plants." In Paris, he nurtures his potted Fatshedra plant and roots bits of kitchen vegetables in little dishes, and he teaches the

Italian's children to grow things. He checks in with
the local animal world too, however, by joining the
ornithologistes. They desire, like Peter, to observe, not
to interfere, and they see birds not spotted in Paris for
fifty years. Peter is inspired to hope that "as the old
haunts of birds were transformed into sinister housing
developments, linked by murderous highways, the
city would become an aviary."

The vision is not far-fetched. Birds are Nature's
survivors, tenacious and adaptable. Sparrows, pigeons,
and multitudinous other birds have long flocked ami-
ably with man; and now falcons have begun to take up
city residence, drawn to the abundant prey of smaller
birds, city mice, and other fauna. Birds are the most
visible of Nature's wild creatures, but Peter's story
begins and ends with captive birds, the melancholy
owl and the violent swan, victims alike of the un-
feathered kind.

It is not always easy to classify this latter kind.
The hawk-faced admiral in Rocky Port is "leaning" to
Goldwater in the 1964 presidential campaign, but he
and his wife constitute the local chapter of the Ban-the-
Bomb organization. In Paris, the American general and
the French colonel are recognizable from their cry for
bombing, but the fledgling Benjy—surely named
for Faulkner's idiot—who has just enlisted and only
hopes that the war will last until he can do some killing, embarrasses even the general with his simple-
minded murderousness. All the Thanksgiving guests
are nonplussed by the pure Roberta's snub of the
ultimate American bird, the flightless all-breasted turkey, purchased frozen at the PX to be the focal point
of the little drama of Americans being thankful for
their conveniences and comforts.

In Rome, Mr. Small observes the habits and plots
the flyways of the common tourist of all nations, as
objectively pleased by what he sees as are the *orni-*

thologistes. Peter recognizes Dr. Pangloss in his adviser, who likes capitalism and mass tourism, who
speaks enthusiastically of processing tourists like any
commodity in bulk, of travel options, art-oriented
groups, value systems. He knows the language of his
field and uses it to praise this best of possible worlds.
He considers the crowds of tourists, "constantly
changing," to be "as exciting as any fresco," but he
has seen little and appreciated less of the Sistine
Chapel, where Peter runs into him. Small is of the "I
know what I like" persuasion: "If art doesn't say
something to me directly, without mediation, I'm not
interested," he says, advising Peter to get rid of his
guidebooks. A "very visual person," he sees "wonderful colors, beautiful forms, marvelous light," but so do
many people whose ocular capacities qualify them as
legally blind.

   Peter, on the other hand, sees and feels deeply. He
tells Mr. Small of an eerie experience with a fresco of
a golden-haired youth representing the tribe of Levi
and wonders whether "it could be atavism that made
me sit . . . under my archetype, till I had to finally
turn around and meet his eye?" His favorite is Borromini; he loves the "downy pennate creatures" everywhere in Borromini's work and the "stars, vegetables,
leaves, acorns, flowers." He senses "coded messages
coming from Mother Nature," and he has an almost
mystical experience upon learning that Borromini was
influenced by the Gothic. Peter loves the Gothic and
he loves Borromini; the discovery that his choices are
"stemming from an inner unity" is an exquisite pleasure. If he does not precisely find that Art and Nature
are the same, certainly his love of art coalesces with
his love of nature, and art serves for him integrating
functions. It identifies; it affirms the kinship of man
to nature; it expresses the continuity and community
of human experience. Realizing that Michelangelo

knew where the light would fall every morning "as long as the frescoes lasted," Peter feels "joyful, as when somebody kept a promise."

Peter prefers both art and nature to society, but he honors the bond of common humanity and believes that man, too, is morally bound to nature. Perception of the natural law is the "moral faculty" in man, the "regulatory instinct" that keeps him "in balance with the natural things of the world." But people keep thwarting Peter. In trying to obtain justice for Makowski, he only complicates things for that young man, who is competent to free himself by craft; neither he nor the police share Peter's commitment to justice. And even the more likable Silly declines to be diverted from his dishonorable purposes.

It is the *clocharde*, however, who utterly confounds Peter's philosophy. Bringing her to his "little kingdom," he is apprehensive for his small collection of objects of art and nature and domesticity, but he could bear their destruction by, say, a puppy, if he should bring one home with him. What he fears is loss of "sovereignty," and the literal accuracy of his perception is borne out by the woman's theft of the doorknob, the device which guards access and egress. Peter's sovereignty in his mental kingdom, however, makes him assume that she has in common with him the moral faculty, but there is no evidence of it. She is wordless, filthy, responsive only to wine. Either there is no freedom of will, Peter thinks, or she has chosen her "grisly state." If the latter, then "the will's objects were not the same for everybody. Either way, everything he cared about fell to pieces."

This shattering episode is prelude to the news about the bombing, which brings Peter to despair. He seeks comfort in nature, but the desolation of the zoo only confirms his bereavement. The derelict botanical gardens look like a cemetery, and the vegetable king-

dom is further reduced to the "curious exhibit" of a
cross-section of a giant California sequoia, its growth
rings marked to show its age at the time of milestones
in human history—the birth of Christ, the destruction
of Pompeii. After seeing these monuments to mortal
man's husbandry and being attacked by the black
swan, Peter can only conclude that their common
mother, Nature, is dead: no regulatory instinct is at
work when mechanical American birds drop death on
helpless people.

Peter's peregrinations have shown him a world
reeling with the old burdens of injustice, poverty, and
violence; and none of the old remedies avail. The diehard Catholic priests in Rocky Port see to it that cakes
are still made from scratch for the fair, and Peter loves
the churches of Europe, but there is no hope of salvation through religion. Peter's experience with the
overenrolled, undertaught classes at the Sorbonne is no
endorsement of mass education as an ameliorating influence, and Mr. Small's advice and example are very
small indeed. Science is more destructive than creative; along with vacuum cleaners and flush toilets, of
which Rosamund approves, it has contributed the
traffic of Paris and the bombs dropped on North Vietnam. Revolutions fought against injustice are part of
the history which produced the systematic oppression
of the American Negro and the casual poverty of the
Parisian beggars and *clochards*.

But social progress, when it does occur, is destructive, cutting off the old consolations of nature
and art and severing connections to the past. Rocky
Port claims to be "more democratic" since it has
turned itself into a museum, but nature is driven out,
and now that the village is marketing its traditions,
Peter can see little worth preserving. The historic
markers on the old houses break the long tradition of

simple habitation by making them exhibits. Peter is still willing to sacrifice for equality, in theory, at least, in Rocky Port, and even in Paris, where, though the headless statues pain him, he wonders whether the revolutionaries should not have beheaded language too, another preserver of ancient injustice with its laudatory words—like "noble" or "gentle" or "free"—rooted in a history of social classes. It is only in Rome that Peter faces his dilemma. "When I'm in the Sistine Chapel," he tells Mr. Small, "I hate my fellow man."

Trying to work out a solution, Peter imagines examinations as a means of rationing access to works of art but runs headlong to the conclusion that, in an ideal society, everybody would be educated and class tourists would outnumber even the mass tourists of the real. Even a well-wrought socialist state no longer seems utopian.

Peter and his philosophies are anachronistic; he recognized his quixotic nature in naming his motor-bike for Quixote's nag, but he almost never rides Rosinante any more. A nearer literary relative than the Don is Candide, and perhaps Peter too will have to content himself by cultivating his garden. The phrase "*cultiver leur jardin*" falls from the lips of a woman explaining to Peter why people come to Rocky Port: They want to do the things "they really enjoy"—in other words, to wear flowered Bermuda shorts, lounge on their yachts, and stupefy themselves with martinis. It is not precisely the picture that Voltaire paints at the end of *Candide*:

—Let's work without speculating, said Martin; it's the only way of rendering life bearable.
The whole little group entered into this laudable scheme; each one began to exercise his talents. The little plot yielded fine crops. Cunégonde . . . became an excellent pastry cook. Paquette took up embroidery. . . .[1]

Voltaire's little company sound, as a matter of fact, a lot like Rosamund.

Rosamund defends her domestic economies as a contact with reality, and so they are, with the fruit and the labor which go into home-made jelly. The title of the first chapter, "Winter Visitors," is taken from *Walden*, and Peter naturally thinks of Thoreau as he settles into the "cosy" New England jail. But living simply is time-consuming and undemocratic in these times, and downright expensive if one must buy jelly and throw it away in order to get jelly glasses, as Rosamund threatens to do, or even drive to the county seat for them, as she does.

Rosamund cultivates her garden in a style which is a contact not with contemporary reality but with the past, both real and idealized. The past in Rocky Port, even more the mythic past in Marietta, Ohio, are the Golden Age of Peter's childhood and his mother's in the *real* America. Peter likes to hear about her small-town childhood, but he has "got her to confess that out in Marietta . . . they had had balls and lights on the tree as well as ketchup in the pantry."

Rosamund creates tradition, and she turns everything into a game, "with rules, of course." She has a cocktail before dinner, sitting before the fire; it would not occur to her to drink in the kitchen as she cooks, the way other mothers do. She loves ceremony, abhors substitutions, and believes in sacrifice. Peter is annoyed by her habit of leaving their belongings when she leaves her husbands, but she insists on sacrificing for her freedom—no matter that she buys replacements for the abandoned possessions—and she regrets that Peter's father pays for Peter's support.

Hers is the song of the harpsichord, an elite instrument. She is politically liberal, as Peter is, but he worries because her support of Lyndon Johnson rests in part upon the fact that at least he was a teacher, whereas Goldwater ran a department store. She does not seek political involvement; when she clashes with the police and makes jailbirds of herself and her son, it is on a point of style. We know her from way back when, but for the first time we are seeing her as a comic character, an effect of seeing her through Peter's eyes:

we are the hero of our own story. . . . Our view of others, on the contrary, cannot but be objective and therefore tinged with a sad sense of comedy. Others are to us like the "characters" of fiction, eternal and incorrigible; the surprises they give us turn out in the end to have been predictable—unexpected variations on the theme of being themselves, of the *principio individuationis*.

("Characters in Fiction," *On the Contrary*)

Music, she tells Peter on Valentine's Day, is not political, as he argues that, now that the bombing has begun, she cannot represent the government committing that act by touring Poland under the auspices of the State Department. He knows, however, that she will, after thinking it over, cancel the tour. "What shook him was that it should have taken her nineteen-year-old son to make plain to her that there were things she could not do."

But the prohibition against touring Poland does not exist in nature, and it is not an immediately apparent consequence of applying the categorical imperative. It is a law of Peter's making, and Peter Levi, by name rooted in the priestly traditions of Christianity and Judaism, earthbound pilgrim and student of mankind, is qualified to make laws. He has been doing it all along. He was mistaken about Nature. Although the announcement of her death is made by Kant, the delirium is Peter's and the conclusion too is his. Mother Nature depends upon rather than provides man's regulatory instinct, an unsettling fact of the human condi-

tion. Nature is a victim of that busy monster man-
*un*kind—unnatural—and her condition is grave, but
when she dies, man dies. His link to Nature is mutual
dependence; his moral laws, if any, are of his own
making.

   Birds of America is a McCarthy anthology, har-
boring between its covers what might be called digres-
sions on diverse subjects—Vietnam, the character of
the French, art, among others—that interest her hero
because they interest her. The purposes of the social
critic sometimes override those of the novelist, and
this must be acknowledged as a defect. Even conced-
ing that the authorial digression is firmly established in
the novel's history and that a book which is not altogether a novel can still be a good book, *Birds of America* is not a very good book. It is an excellent, funny,
tender story—the Rocky Port adventure—followed
by a series of scenes and essays containing a procession
of characters who verge on the allegorical and a conclusion which, although bringing together the main
threads of the book, is contrived.

8

~.~.~.~.~.~.~.~.~.~.~.~.~.~.~.~.~.~.

The Author in Her Own Voice
Essays on Diverse Subjects

Alfred Kazin has called Mary McCarthy a "brilliant culture critic,"[1] and so she is. She is not much of a theorist; she does not write about Communism, for example, but about Communists. The abstraction interests her as it relates to practical affairs, and the word "culture" is used here in its broad sense, including not only literature and art but also such practical affairs as the conduct of war and the application of justice.

This chapter will examine *Venice Observed* as an example of McCarthy's contribution to nonfiction *belles lettres* and her essays on Vietnam and Watergate as examples of her social criticism. They are, however, more than examples, each being uniquely successful and therefore important. By devoting this chapter to these works, I am skipping a scattering of short stories: "An Unspoiled Reaction," an unrepresentative story about the breakdown of a puppeteer at a children's matinee, and "The Weeds" (*Cast a Cold Eye*), a dreary story about a Margaret-like woman who leaves her husband and comes back to him, to name two. "The Appalachian Revolution" and "The Hounds of Summer" are more regrettable omissions. I have mentioned in passing some of the most important essays, but not the many fine literary essays on individual writers such as Dickens, Flaubert, Compton-

Burnett, Burroughs, Orwell, Sarraute, and Shakespeare.
(She particularly dislikes Salinger and greatly admires Dickens, Tolstoy, and Nabokov.) She rarely
writes about popular culture, but in "Up the Ladder
from *Charm* to *Vogue*" she analyzes the fashion magazines' condescension toward their readers, who require
a good deal of spit and polish as well as advice in order
to be made at all presentable.

Most of McCarthy's nonfiction, like most of her
fiction, is quite personal. Travel literature, dependent
as it is on the author's personality, can be loosely clas-
sified as autobiography. Since McCarthy is extraordinarily observant and unfailingly concrete, it is not
surprising that her travel pieces are masterful, whether
their angle is descriptive and academic, as in *Venice
Observed* and *The Stones of Florence*, or argumentative and political, as in *Vietnam* and *Hanoi*, or both, as
in the essays on Lisbon (in *On the Contrary*). When
McCarthy writes about a place, she tells us what to
make of it. She is as good at characterizing cities as she
is with people, at finding, as Barbara McKenzie calls it
in *Mary McCarthy*, the key that works the city.

McCarthy particularly enjoyed writing the Venice and Florence books, she says, because she spoke in
her own voice rather than through a character. In
spite of the research required, she wrote them very
quickly. The pleasure is evident, but not the haste.
Venice is, McCarthy tells us, "a game, a fantasy, a
fable," everything in it designed to catch the eye and
the ear, everyone in it ready to drop what he is doing
and act as a guide. *Venice Observed* is written in a
style exquisitely suited to the subject, one that has
long attracted literary travelers, so that figuratively as
well as literally

No stones are so trite as those of Venice, that is, precisely,
so well worn. It has been part museum, part amusement

park, living off the entrance fees of tourists, ever since the early eighteenth century, when its former sources of revenue ran dry.

Unreality and illusion give Venice much of its beauty; the marble veneers of St. Mark's,

especially when washed by the rain so that they look like oiled silk, are among the most beautiful things in Venice. And it is their very thinness, the sense they give of being a mere lustrous coating, a film, that makes them beautiful. A palace of solid marble, rain washed, simply looks bedraggled.

As a whole, St. Mark's "is not beautiful, and yet again it is. . . . And it can take you unawares. . . ."

The "inherent improbability" of everything in Venice is symbolized by the gondola, "floating, insubstantial, at once romantic and haunting, charming and absurd." Traffic lights, McCarthy writes,

are not funny, but it is funny to have one in Venice over a canal-intersection. . . . The things of *this* world reveal their essential absurdity when they are put in the Venetian context.

Much of Venetian history, however, is grim; and even in its improbable present, the "charming scene" of "silent rows of little girls in smocks" making lace in Burano does not withstand close scrutiny, for the children work an eight-hour day for about 64 cents on lace that will sell for "very high prices" in the shops of Venice.

McCarthy finds Venetian painting to be marked by a "reverence for the concrete world." The rich materials known to the old merchants are "one aspect of the continuity of Venetian painting," which is "from beginning to end a riot of dress goods." The concrete world embraces all manner of birds and beasts and men, however.

It would be false to say that Venetian painting embodied a democratic tendency, and yet that is the impression made on me by Giovanni Bellini, Cima, the Bastiani, Basaiti, and—later—Tintoretto. The company of saints appears as a community of equals, sandalled pioneers of a model Republic, whose women folk could afford the latest styles in dress. This is a republic which includes the animal kingdom—an ark, you might say.

The text amounts to only 158 pages in paperback, yet it contains a wealth of information; leafing through, one is astonished to realize that it bristles with dates, names, and facts, for its effect is by turns lyrical, dramatic, and comic. The latter quality is provided chiefly in the account of McCarthy's living arrangment, which she describes early and returns to near the end, thus using it as a bridge between the illusion of Venice and the reality of daily life.

Despite a bathroom to be shared with her landlady's family, McCarthy is promised privacy by the rental agent. But soon a cat makes its presence known by clawing at her apartment window, a "displaced person" like the invisible signore put out for the period while the apartment is rented. *"Permesso,"* says the signora, "bursting" into the sitting room to thrust food out the window to the animal: *"Poverino."* By the last pages of the book, McCarthy reports that the entire family have "slowly, like cats, repossessed their apartment, corner by corner, room by room. . . . One day, the bathtub is full of laundry. . . . My toilet soap vanishes, as if by magic. . . . I find I have to buy a fresh box of powder. A guest comes to stay with me, and the signora takes her aside, to ask her, *per piacere,* where she buys her toothpaste. 'Mario *loves* it!' she declares, alluding to her son."

The signora's groceries "invade" McCarthy's icebox, an ironing board appears in her ktichen; and gradually the family becomes "established around the kitchen table. . . ." Strangers appear with clothes and jewelry, and the signora brings in paintings: "Does she expect me to buy them . . . ?" When no interest is shown, the items disappear.

The furniture and trappings of the apartment are all in a state of flux—here today, gone tomorrow. Nothing is anchored to its place, not even the coffee-pot, which floats off and returns, on the tide of the signora's marine nature.

The metaphor is typical of the rich preciseness of the book's style. Near the beginning, McCarthy writes that the "hale old doges and warriors" of Venetian history "seem to us a strange breed of sea-animal who left behind them the pink, convoluted shell they grew to protect them, which is Venice." The shell, the signora's starving goldfish, the republic that is "an ark, you might say," are part of a flow of animal and watery images with which McCarthy describes the shimmering city in all its fabulous absurdity, until at last, "I shall have to go soon, I dreamily realize, or I shall come back one day to the apartment to find that *I* have vanished, following my soap and perfume. . . ." She will have to go by gondola because she has so much baggage. And, she concludes,

That is how the Allies took Venice, arriving from the mainland, at the end of the second World War. There was a petrol shortage, and the Allied command, having made secret contact with the gondoliers' co-operative, officially "captured" Venice with a fleet of gondolas. Even war in Venice evokes a disbelieving smile.

McCarthy is never too much enchanted, however, to look beneath a beautiful surface; what is past is past, but the little lace makers prompt her to questions about their eyesight and to a fruitless effort to learn who profits from their labors. They become a touchstone by which she assesses other descriptions of Venice because no writer who can be trusted would be simply charmed by the sight of these exploited children.

In "Mlle. Gulliver en Amérique," McCarthy makes it clear not only what she dislikes about Simone de Beauvior but what she demands of writers in general. Mlle. de Beauvior is careless; she "speaks repeatedly of James Algee (Agee), of Farrel (Farrell), O'Neil (O'Neill), and of Max Twain," as well as of "Greeniwich" Village. But worse, she believes whatever she is told that confirms her preconceptions: that American literary magazines print only favorable reviews, that American private schools pay their faculty better than state schools, and the like. What vexes McCarthy is the absence of an "investigative instinct" to check such reports for accuracy before writing them as fact (which of course they are not).

McCarthy herself has the investigative instinct; the communication between fact and fiction in her writing is direct, but the distinction is clear. She twice went on fact-finding missions to Vietnam; she sends a group of fictional characters on a fact-finding mission in her latest novel, *Cannibals and Missionaries*. Some of the sources for the novel are evident in her account of the backgrounds of her trips to Vietnam.

She has long been an analyst of the American character and, like Peter Levi, a lover of America. If she came near despair on her country's behalf during the Vietnam War and its aftermath, she took heart again in the intellectualization of the country that she saw in traveling across it during the Watergate hearings, when housewives rearranged schedules and forgot about soap operas to follow this complicated business on their televisions, cab drivers kept their radios tuned to the hearings, and everybody was full of names and dates and opinions. This was a moral crisis which engaged the national attention—except, McCarthy concedes, for a few people, wealthy in her experience, who professed a disdain for the whole matter.

The Vietnam essays, most of them published first as periodical articles, appeared as pamphlets, and then in 1974 were collected and again republished with the addition of an autobiographical essay, "How It Went," and a review of David Halberstam's book *Sons of the Morning* in *The Seventeenth Degree* (1974). "How It Went" is McCarthy at her most personal, writing about her daily affairs and her conscience. It narrates the background of her two trips to Vietnam, provides a glimpse at her fourth marriage, and expresses the intensity of her opposition to America's activities in Vietnam:

> . . . I did an interview with Edwin Newman [1966] in Paris during which I said that if Americans did not act against the war, put down some real stake, our case would not be so different from that of the "good" Germans under Hitler who claimed to have disagreed with the Final Solution, offering as proof the fact that they had taken no active part in it.

The American bombing of North Vietnam had come as a shock to McCarthy, and she immediately sought ways to do something about it. She found that, although the war had many eminent critics in various fields, few possessors of the "names" that she needed to form the nucleus of a protest movement were willing to be inconvenienced. Her opportunity to do something came in the form of an invitation to go to Vietnam for the *New York Review of Books*.

"I confess that when I went to Vietnam early last February I was looking for material damaging to the American interest. . . ." begins her first article. McCarthy's angle is cultural. There are accounts of American and South Vietnamese corruption and of atrocities still painful to contemplate, but for the most part she emphasizes the misguided and self-deceived efforts of Americans to bestow their way of life on the unwilling inhabitants of Vietnam. The American mission is to spread American values

until everyone is convinced, by demonstration, that the American way is better, just as American seed strains are better and American pigs are better. [This] conviction is sometimes baldly stated. . . . Or it may wear a humanitarian disguise, *e.g.*, Operation Concern, in which a proud little town in Kansas airlifted 110 pregnant sows to a humble little town in Vietnam.

Saigon "resembles a gigantic PX," a "stewing Los Angeles," a "World's Fair or Exposition in some hick American city." Poverty and vice inhabit the streets. Whole families cook their meals there and sleep amid the filth.

The Americans—by bombing the countryside and destroying villages and crops to leave nothing of value to the enemy—have created a homeless peasantry. But thereby they have provided themselves with "congenial" channels for the exercise of diverse talents other than the merely destructive ones. New hamlets are planned. Youth affairs and urban development agencies are created. An official "rubs his hands with pleasure: 'First we organized it *vertically*. Now we've organized it horizontally.' " Medical teams meet the challenge of public health with temporary clinics set up to inform the peasants that they are tubercular, to vaccinate and immunize them, to teach them hygiene and, where necessary, to "nurse them back to health"—but not all of them, since hospital facilities are inadequate. Some of the burned children, of course, would not need medical attention except for the American military presence, and the medical miracles are further compromised when malnourished children, nursed—or fed—back to health, are sent home to their impoverished parents to go hungry again.

At a refugee camp which is a "showcase" for the application of American know-how and good will to the displaced Vietnamese, an official complains about a journalist's report that a resident of Phu Cuong wished that she were dead. " 'But that's natural.' I objected. 'Her husband had been killed by the Americans, and she'd lost her home and everything she had.' " The American nonetheless protests the "unfair" suggestion that the Vietnamese refugees are not altogether happy. "This lunatic attitude is widespread, though not always so doggedly stated." Phu Cuong, for all its fresh water, sanitation, and generous provisions, is, McCarthy observes, a concentration camp. And it is, as far as she can tell, unique. She finds other refugee establishments and a leper house in Hue unspeakably filthy.

As Americans work at their color-coded maps, charting the relocations of the powerless Vietnamese, they chart whole new vocabularies as well, redefining words like "constructed" and "reconstructed" and inventing ones like "infrastructure," while at the same time disdaining semantics. A military spokesman, asked to clarify a statement, coldy declines to debate "semantics" with the questioner. And by a semantic coup, serious problems are solved; enemy actions are "atrocities," but apparent American atrocities are "accidents."

But in what way accidental if the fliers saw the village and could assume that there were people in it and knew from experience that the bombs would go off? Well, the fliers were really aiming at the Viet Cong; if they hit some civilians, that was unintentional—it just happened.

McCarthy urges the withdrawal of American troops from Vietnam. She raises the anguished question of an honorable and orderly exit in order to answer it bluntly: there is "no honorable exit from a shameful course of action." The error of those who

offer helpful suggestions about how to get out is the
assumption that *how* is a fundamental problem. Even
the liberal opposition to the war itself is confounded
by the matter of *how*. That, McCarthy says, is the
business of the politcians, who can manage very well.
The business of intellectuals is to make it clear that
they must.

At the heart of all three Vietnam pieces—four,
counting the review of *Sons of the Morning*—is an
insistence on freedom to act, an all but forgotten con-
cept in America. President Johnson feels that he has
no choice in the conduct of the war. If there is a
"certain psychological truth" in his conviction that he
is not free to act—to stop the bombing, for example—
it is because

Johnson and his advisers, like all Americans, are the con-
ditioned subjects of the free-enterprise system. . . . A sense
of compulsion, dictated by the laws of the market, per-
meates every nerve of the national life.

Freedom, McCarthy continues, is not treated as a
"political value" in America but rather as "the right to
self-expression," and opposition to the war is a minority pastime, tolerated by a majority which can
afford dissent and ignored by the administration. (We
should remember that when McCarthy was writing
this, the Kent State killings were still in the future.)
But if the opposition would, it could find ways to
make itself hard to ignore. The conclusion of *Vietnam*
calls for putting up a stake, for "From each according
to his abilities, but to be in the town jail, as Thoreau
knew, can relieve any sense of imaginary imprison-
ment."

McCarthy was not, of course, unique in calling
for American withdrawal from Vietnam, nor was
Diana Trilling unique among opponents of the war in
her objection to our simply pulling out (published in

the *New York Review of Books* in response to Mc-
Carthy, and reprinted along with McCarthy's reply as a
preface to *Hanoi*). Trilling argues that simple withdrawal would "consign untold numbers of Southeast
Asian opponents of Communism to their death and
countless more to the abrogation of the right of protest which we American intellectuals hold so dear."

McCarthy is characteristically rational. She writes
that, not having the gift of prophecy, she does not
know that two million people would die without
American protection. But short of annexing Vietnam,
thus "*imposing* democratic institutions on the South
Vietnamese" and making the war a legitimate American concern because it would be "taking place on U.S.
soil," she can think of no solution giving "ironclad
permanent protection to untold numbers of anti-
Communists." If we do not want to do that, we seem
obliged to continue the war "along present lines, reg-
ularly escalating until all resistance has been eliminated
or until our computers tell us that two million and one
innocent persons have been killed—at that point the
war would no longer be 'worth it,' and we could quit
with a clear conscience." McCarthy does not hold the
conviction of some people that opposing Communism
at any cost is a moral imperative; "the alternatives to
Communism offered by the Western countries are all
ugly in their own ways and getting uglier."

In *Hanoi*, McCarthy shares with the North Vietnamese the risk of being hit by an American bomb. "I
could not bear to see my country disfigure itself so,
when I might do something to stop it. It had surprised
me to find that I cared enough about America to risk
being hit by a U.S. bomb for its sake. . . ." There are
uneasy moments in North Vietnam—the attack alerts,
when she is whisked to shelters, or the crossing of a
bridge, inch by inch, in the knowledge that there are
not any shelters between the banks of the river—but

there are no hair-raising narrow escapes. The immediate area of her hotel is probably safe, unless the administration "escalated again, with B-two's or 'nukes,' in which case my personal survival was not of any interest; I would not care to survive."

Hanoi, she finds, is "a shady, leafy city, like Minneapolis or Warsaw." A bomb-blasted tree putting out new leaves is, to the North Vietnamese, a symbol: "All of Nature is with them, not just the 'brother socialist countries.'" In appearance and even in comfort (there is plenty of hot water in her hotel, a luxury she did not enjoy in Saigon), Hanoi is more pleasant than Saigon, except for the attack alerts and the cylindrical man-sized bomb shelters everywhere, waiting to be sunk into holes. Though poor, North Vietnam is clean, hardworking, and vice-free. McCarthy is alert to the possibility that her impressions are manipulated, but she sees nothing to contradict the official presentation of North Vietnamese life.

There is abundant visible evidence to refute the American claim that the bombing is limited to military and strategic targets. A model leper colony—the surviving lepers, of course, have had to be moved—has, inexplicably, been hit not just once but thirty-nine times. The North Vietnamese are aware, however, that American policy does not reflect the unified will of Americans, and they accept McCarthy quite simply as a friend. They even give her the mementos popular among themselves, presenting her with a ring and a comb made from downed U.S. bombers.

Perhaps, if I had had the courage, I might have declined. . . . But from their point of view, [the ring] was a symbol of friendship. . . . What was it that, deeper than politeness, which was urging me to do so, made it impossible to keep it on my finger, even for a few minutes—just not to give offense?

She takes note a certain caution, a rationing of ideas, among her hosts, which she attributes to the requirement of unity imposed by the American threat. And language, here as in the South, is difficult. "One cannot use language as a sort of reversible raincoat, wearing the side out that is best suited to the political climate where one happens to be at the time." She is accustomed to use "Viet Cong" as a "normal straightforward term for the insurgent forces in the South," but in the North, the term is "impermissible": "Cong" is "Communist," and the North Vietnamese deny Communist "leadership and inspiration" in the movement. "The People's Liberation Army" is the correct term in the North.

Maybe it is a literary prejudice to dislike such words as "free" and "people" when what they refer to is uncertain. When Johnson talks about "the American people," he means the supporters of his war policy, and when the North Vietnamese talk about "the American people" as against "the Johnson clique," they mean the opposite.

McCarthy has vowed to herself not to speak of "the puppet government" of Thieu and Ky, a phrase which she can hear with equanimity from her hosts but which impedes conversation. She cannot refer to the "South Vietnamese government" in a discussion of the "puppet government" when the point of her companions is that the government in question is not a government but a tool.

It is quite possible to say or write "The Saigon government is a puppet of the United States." Agreed. But to reiterate the notion every hour on the hour . . . awakens the critical spirit. . . . A figure of speech, overworked, takes its revenge by coming to life, and you wonder who is the puppet, the Arvin soldier or the orator who does not tire of calling him that, mechanically, like a recording.

McCarthy questions her "bourgeois individual-
ism" in desiring to construct her phrases rather than
take them ready-made; in our society, she says, "orig-
inality has become a sort of fringe benefit, a *mere*
convention." She is not exempt from the convention,
however, and her difficulty in discussing political subjects in language offensive neither to herself nor her
hosts leads her often to questions about the "flora and
fauna of the regions through which we were driving"
and provides her with a transition to a discussion of
the land itself.

She finds the North Vietnamese "propaganda" tir-
ing but not untrue: "One-sided, you might argue, except that in my opinion the Americans do not *have* a
side in this war." Other sympathetic Americans grow
weary of the repetition: "Are they still harping on
that leper colony?" one asks McCarthy. But as the
North Vietnamese "harp" on their themes of "war
and defiance," the "U. S. policy, unvarying in content,
has been clothed in seasonal changes of words as the
years have rolled by." Johnson "limits" the bombing in
his speeches while increasing it in reality.

McCarthy is only occasionally discomfited by the
distance, or rather the angles, between herself and her
hosts, but she is less at ease with the two American
prisoners of war whom she is allowed to interview. She
and the pilots quickly run through the obligatory
topics—"Health," "Family," "Treatment" "Current
View of the War"—and the "sole question" put to her
by the younger of the men is, "Can you tell me how
the Chicago Cubs are doing?" She does not record her
reply. In the distance between herself and these men
she reads "a crime against humanity, a reason for protest, for revolutions," while acknowledging that to
the pilots she probably seemed a "tool" of the North
Vietnamese, "shaped by Eastern education, money,
advantages." Opposition to the war she recognizes as

"an economic privilege enjoyed chiefly by the middle and professional classes," and she is frankly "more at home talking French with Dr. Ton That Tung, say, on medical and philosophical subjects than making lame conversation in English with those wary cagey pilots about hobbies, church, family, and the American primary elections."

Seeing little to be proud of about her country, McCarthy has "joyed" in the freedom to write, but in Hanoi, for the first time, she finds that freedom regarded as "just another capitalist luxury." And she suggests that freedom of information, when not effective in promoting action, "may actually be unhealthy, like any persistent frustration, for a body politic." As "the illusion of being effective" fails her, McCarthy becomes self-critical:

My objectivity was making me uncomfortable, like a trade mark or shingle advertising a genuine Mary McCarthy product ("Trust Her to Speak Her Mind"). In short, I was not pleased with myself, or with what I somewhat showily represented.

The Catholic girl has survived with scruples and honesty intact. Musing that her "private tumults and crises" center upon "trivial" occasions—the gift of the ring, the avoidance of the word "puppet"—McCarthy recognizes that these things matter because of the "ubiquity of God. . . . Being an unbeliever made no difference. . . . What remained from my Catholic training was the idea that it was necessary to be the same person at all times and places."

In her personal unity, she finds resistance to the reporter's mission: "you ought not to be two people, one downstairs, listening and nodding, and the other scribbling in your room." The North Vietnamese, she assumes, would not scruple against "drawing up a full report every evening," for their ethic is public—"in the service of the state"—and hers is "more selfish, mainly working at my own salvation." Although "in practice the results may look similar," McCarthy finds her quest for salvation less than admirable. Apart from patriotism, her motive, she confesses, is to resume her "normal pursuits. Reading, writing, spending money, looking at pictures and cathedrals, entertaining friends. Sleeping. Paying my income tax. I was still doing all those things, except sleeping, pretty much as formerly, but with a disturbed conscience . . . and hence without pleasure."

But "Nothing will be the same again, if only because of the awful self-recognitions, including this one, the war has enforced." It is clear that McCarthy found the North Vietnamese experience jarring. South Vietnam was easier. The purpose of that visit was easier to define, the risk easier to calculate, the intellectual, linguistic, and sociological climate familiar. The ugly American is fair game, and every half-serious American writer has taken a shot or two at him. And whatever she received of assistance or hospitality in Saigon, no matter how gratefully, was owed her as an American reporter, no matter how "risible" the idea of a war correspondent for the *New York Review of Books.*

In Hanoi she is an honored guest. Ceremoniously entertained in a poor, unoffending country being bombed by the most powerful nation in the world, she takes a cold look at herself. She is not here to judge *them.* The Prime Minister, impressed by what he has read in French of her book on South Vietnam, hopes that she will write a book about the North. "It would depend on how much material I had. 'I can't make a book out of something that isn't one,' " she tells him. She is relieved to hear later that she has not given offense by "this stiffening of artistic integrity," that the Prime Minister approves of her honesty.

This, then, was the universal pardon. I was set free. . . .
The North Vietnamese did not expect more of me than
what I was. From each according to his abilities, which is
the same as saying, in my Father's house, there are many
mansions.

And so Marx and Jesus are in accord.

Hanoi ends with an account of McCarthy's in-
quiries about a German doctor and his wife who fear-
lessly drove along roads where others dared not pass,
treating whatever sick and wounded they found. Reports are that they may have been killed by the Viet
Cong or the North Vietnamese; a young leftist remarks that "What happened to them was their own
fault for trying to be disinterested do-gooders. *'Plus
ou moins sympathiques'* was insufficient." Such views
McCarthy finds far from the North Vietnamese
"principle of limit" but close to the American view
according to which "anybody who remains in a hamlet designated Viet Cong is liable to execution from
the air. Our position is that they got what was coming
to them for sticking around."

The killing of civilians by either side is indefen-
sible, but there is little to equalize the guilt in this
atrocity, if there was one—the fate of the Krainicks
remains unknown—because there were so many au-
thenticated ones on our side that the mention of the
Krainicks seems almost gratuitous. That, of course, is
McCarthy's point.

McCarthy has a well-trained and sophisticated
mind, but like Martha Sinnott, she possesses a clarity
of mind that leads her to simple observations:

Either it is morally wrong for the United States to bomb
a small and virtually defenseless country or it is not, and a
student picketing the Pentagon is just as great an expert in
that realm, to say the least, as Dean Rusk or Joseph Alsop.

But she does not spare the student picketing the Pentagon, either, for all his rectitude. She chastizes him in
Medina.

The self-persuasion of innocence that accompanied the
American soldier on the road to My Lai [scene of the infamous massacre which led to the court-martials of officers
Calley and Medina] has its counterpart in the self-persuasion of guilt on the part of many young rebels, which they
redistribute, though, to their elders and to the country at
large or, more vaguely, the "system." Where the G.I. in
Vietnam out on patrol felt he was really a civilian that nobody had the right to snipe at, the counter-culture is convinced that all Americans except themselves are war-
makers, *i.e.*, indistinguishable from war criminals.

Such virtuous "indictments" of a whole culture in its
ordinary pursuits are politically sterile.

Small wonder that the Vietnamese books were received in relative silence. They would hardly have
been welcome to the Hawks; but the Doves must have
been taken aback, too, at being held partly responsible
for the outcome of the Medina trial (Calley had been
convicted, his sentence reduced by then-President
Nixon; Medina was acquitted). Americans, McCarthy
observes, were pleased to boast of their country's
uniqueness in putting these men on trial for war
crimes.

Yet that boast was a source of anger to the local "counter-
culture," which grudges this miserable country any point
of pride. . . . Doubtless, if Calley had been acquitted, there
would have been the same storm (cries of "hypocrisy,"
"fake justice") from the left that followed his conviction,
though the right would have been appeased. The result is
now visible. . . . Now any member of the armed forces in
Indochina can, if he desires, slaughter a reasonable number
of babies, confident that the public will acquit him, a) because they support the war and the Army or b) because
they don't.

McCarthy finds the cynicism of the left, which scorned the idea of justice in the military courts, destructive because it effectively relieved the courts of their responsibility to that part of society which should have been most vocal in demanding justice. "Cynicism about 'the system' is a poor guide to political action; it does not matter if the disgusted cynic is 99 per cent right in his estimates."

But I do not mean to imply that "We have seen the enemy and he is us" is the entire burden of *Medina*. McCarthy describes the proceedings in the Georgia courtroom and reconstructs the crime from the testimony. Her emphasis is upon facts: where Medina was, what he was doing, what he must have heard and could or should have seen from his vantage point, what he failed to do. He was acquitted on a technicality, but in no sense was he shown to be innocent of responsibility for the killing of some one hundred civilians in the Vietnamese village. McCarthy is not to be distracted by arguments about relative responsibility along the chain of command.

Her journalistic objectivity is reserved for the search for truth. She is not objective toward people who can be judged by their actions. Never has her novelist's eye been more coldly cast than upon Medina and his defenders, particularly his counsel, F. Lee Bailey, here on display for anyone interested in seeing one of our most successful lawyers at work. *Medina* is a very harsh book. America was past the excuse of self-deception. The My Lai massacre was fully and publicly documented, and virtually nothing was done about it.

The Senate Watergate committee investigated a different kind of crime, a more elusive and subtle evil. Since few facts were ascertainable, McCarthy in *The Mask of State* emphasizes character. The proceedings

from time to time take on the allegorical dimensions of
a morality play:

Perhaps [John D. Ehrlichman] cannot help his face, but
he looks like somebody of a deeply criminal nature, out of
a medieval fresco: the upward sneering curl of the left-
hand side of the mouth matched, on the bias, by the upward lift of the right eyebrow. . . . the aggressive tilted
nose that cameramen say has been growing all week, the
sinister (literally) thrust of the jaw. Everything about his
features and body movements is canted, tilted, slanting,
sloping, askew.

The portraits are devastating, but there is an
undercurrent of hope in McCarthy's interpretation of
the events which she describes with an acid pen; led
by Senator Ervin, the committee is determinedly seeking the truth about the Watergate break-in, and the
country is alert and informed. This is a moral crisis,
and responsible action is being taken. She fears for the
outcome, but she finds much to approve of in the
works of the Ervin committee.

The drama is full of villains, but perhaps the most
memorable portrait is of John Mitchell, "that feral old
dog." He probably did not, McCarthy decides, have
anything to do with the break-in, an idea too foolish
and unproductive to have had his approval, let alone
his authorization; and he was probably drawn into the
cover-up by loyalty to Nixon, a quality which does
nothing to redeem him. Reflecting that the committee's efforts to get truth from Mitchell are like trying
to get blood from a turnip, McCarthy explores the
metaphor: "indeed there was something turnipy about
Mitchell, the off-white (or tattletale gray) face with
occasional mottlings of purplish pink, the watery,
squelchy voice, the smooth bald pate." Insolently un-
communicative, Mitchell is nonetheless the one who
finally, almost incidentally, provides a glimpse into the
heart of the darkness in which Watergate took form.

Senator Baker: "What is your perception of the institution of the Presidency?" Mitchell allowed that that would take a long time to answer, but then answers started popping out of him like sulphurous firecrackers. His perception of the institution was that he was unable to contemplate anybody but Richard Nixon in it, as though the presidency had become unique with Nixon's incumbency, different from anything previous and requiring self-succession. . . . He now went on to say, with a brief verbal genuflection. . . . [that] He himself had spared [Nixon] knowledge of the "horror stories" and incidentally Watergate . . . to relieve him of the need to decide what to do about them.

Making decisions "would have impeded his potential for re-election," and Mitchell "was not about to countenance anything that would hinder that re-election." He seemed unaware, McCarthy writes, "of the enormity of what he was enunciating—a doctrine of a higher law transcending the Constitution, incarnate in the figure of our old friend Tricky Dick." There is nothing about "*policies* that might call for continuance," merely an insistence on the "person of Nixon (whom he also referred to as 'the individual'), whose sole function seemed to be getting re-elected, like a perpetual motion machine."

Behind this "proto-fascist mentality" McCarthy sees the spectre of totalitarianism. The disparity between the circumstances and the people involved, including this turnipy individual "pulling at its pipe," is jolting. The style is what brings us up short, as the sentence rolls with ponderous formality through "enormity," "enunciating," "transcending," "incarnate," and on to the anticlimax of "our old friend Tricky Dick," the incarnation before whom the "verbal genuflection" has taken place, the self-justifying perpetual motion machine.

Watergate had its light as well as its dark comedy, most notably in the "Keystone-comedy cop Tony

Ulasewicz," the Sancho Panza to Kalmbach, who, "belonging to a softer breed . . . could never have carried ten-dollar bills amounting to $50,000 around in brown paper bags tied with little pieces of string. . . . would never have thought of a bus-driver's metal money-changer to store coins for pay telephones. . . ." Coping with large amounts of cash to be paid as "legal fees" to the men arrested for the break-in provided Ulasewicz with "suspense-filled adventures, which were rather like a Harold Lloyd comedy. . . . Through him, and picturing him as a partner, one could even sympathize a little with Kalmbach."

The hero of the affair was, of course, Senator Ervin, in his role as country lawyer an actor "virtually Shakespearean, and showing the bard's own fondness for character parts and honest common-sense rustics. In these hearings, Senator Ervin represents the humble, 'low' reality principle and has clearly chosen to do so, which is why the audience loves him." When Jeb Stuart Magruder tries to connect his disillusionment with his old ethics professor, the Reverend William Sloan Coffin, who engaged in public illegalities like draft-card burning, to his own participation in the Watergate cover-up, "Senator Ervin, a civil-libertarian, pulled him up sharp. 'Dr. Coffin was just demonstratin', wasn't he?'" Ervin is drawn large as life, the famous eyebrows in motion, with affection and admiration. He is not, however, spared the wart of his hawkishness, to which McCarthy attributes his acceptance of the Stennis compromise on the matter of the tapes, but she remarks that "every good man pays for his sins," as kindly a condemnation as she has ever written.

Writing her last comments several months before the inconclusive finale of these events—Nixon's resignation followed by his pardon from his appointed

successor—McCarthy argues from the "pathology" of
the evidence that Nixon himself authorized the Watergate break-in, of which, given the character of the
administration, the cover-up was merely the inevitable
consequence. It is a convincing argument. We will
probably never know. "It is important, I think," Mc-
Carthy writes, "to realize that Nixon saw nothing
wrong in the conception of governing" through ques-
tionable methods. "To him, control of the IRS was
one of the natural perquisites of office. . . . As for the
wire-tapping of dissenters and subversives, some people, he knew, thought it was illegal, but it was not
wrong. . . ."

No doubt it will be years yet before the question
of legality is settled, for the pardon did not relieve
Nixon of the obligation to answer for his actions in
the civil courts; that obligation is still being tested as
this is written. But Watergate, like Vietnam, is behind
us. McCarthy connects the two episodes in our history, seeing the national involvement in the Watergate affair as part of an urge to be cleansed of guilt for
Vietnam. She points as partial evidence to the active
participation in the Watergate hearings by people who
had supported, or at least not opposed, the war, and
the relative silence of the Doves with their lesser guilt.

And perhaps she is right. But now, having understood nothing, we have forgiven all. The thing is, we
still have Nixon to kick around. The war criminals
and the Watergate gang are back on the streets, having "suffered" enough, and the former president has
expressed the desire for a political job of some ad-
visory sort—which should be a ludicrous idea. Nothing
has been resolved, and the only sense in which these
national crises are behind us is chronological. Those
who supported the war and those who remained loyal
to Nixon have not been refuted.

Ervin, McCarthy writes, was "stubbornly convinced" that the hearings would arrive at the truth about Watergate.

"But if it doesn't come out that way?" I said to him. "If they fail? Just take it as a hypothesis." "I refuse to entertain the thought" was his answer, as though the thought was a felon seeking entry into his mental premises. . . . I hope he is right, but if he is right and nothing then happens—a strong possibility—then we are worse off than we were before. If we know, that is, and don't act, can find no frame for action, Nixon and his sly firm, *knowing* that *we* know and won't do anything, will have nothing more to fear.

The pardon effectively canceled the search for truth, but it is not Nixon—probably—whom we need fear, but his supporters, the ones who never could see what he did that was so bad. We never were able to tell them.

For some of us, it was not necessary to suspend judgment until all the facts were in. We could live with our private certainties. So, as a matter of fact, could everybody, for there were no public certainties, and one certainty was as good as another. Some Watergate offenders went to jail, and so did some draft refusers. The Watergate offenders came out hale and hearty and writing—of all things—novels, assured of publication with a full measure of sales promotion and, of course, lots of money. Some draft refusers won eligibility for a grudging amnesty.

The lesson seems clear. Public protest on moral grounds does not pay, but covert crime in the service of power is a living. The events McCarthy writes about grow out of the American character, or some part of it, that is not behind us. With her investigative instinct and novelist's eye, McCarthy has learned a good deal about that character, and she has written about it with anger, with grief, with humor, and always with wit and intelligence.

9

~.~.~.~.~.~.~.~.~.~.~.~.~.~.~.~.~.~.

The Sons of Adam In and Out
of Eden: *The Oasis* and *Cannibals
and Missionaries*

In her fiction, McCarthy likes to use the small, self-contained, self-made unit of society, such as Jocelyn or New Leeds, as a setting for the examination of a variety of people in relation to a limited world. In two books, she creates an artificial society and shows people in extraordinary circumstances carrying on very much as if they were in the real world, as the Utopians do in *The Oasis* and the hostages do in *Cannibals and Missionaries*. The early *conte philosophique* and McCarthy's most recent novel pit ideals against reality and find man and his institutions impervious.

The Oasis is sometimes called a novel for the sake of convenience, but it is according to its author a *conte philosophique* with a satiric purpose. As Doris Grumbach writes,

Just as there is no plot, no important events that proceed one from another, so there is no development of character or even any real change in the characters. They are satiric portraits, brilliantly placed like precious stones into a setting. Their failures, or what might be termed their sins, are intellectual, their virtues are the negative ones, their attractions for the reader are their patent weaknesses.[1]

And once again, McCarthy is very critical of liberals. When the book came out in 1949, it angered many who recognized themselves not only as types but as individuals impaled on the rapier of McCarthy's wit. Nonetheless, the little book continues to be highly regarded.

Utopia is the oasis, an abandoned resort hotel purchased by a group of about fifty people, most of them intellectuals, as the setting for a social experiment. They regard the community as a retreat from the threat of atomic warfare and a chance at a simpler life than the one they have left behind. The outcome is foreshadowed in the first paragraphs, where, describing the businessman Joe Lockman, who, "honoring [Utopia's] principles of equality and fraternity . . . was nevertheless determined to get more out of it than anybody else," McCarthy observes that "habits die hard."

Even before the "great migration" to the property, factions develop. The realists, chief of whom is Will Taub, justify the experiment on "sheerly practical grounds, as a retreat from atomic warfare, a summer-vacation colony, a novelty in personal relations." If "in their hearts" they hope, as the purists do, for "some millennial outcome . . . the reign of justice and happiness," they have no conviction that isolation, nearness to nature, a simple life, and the good example of some of the Utopians will bring about moral reform. Nonetheless, they are as determined as the purists are to give the experiment every opportunity to succeed.

And so they set about cultivating their garden, quite literally. Taub soon feels called to more important work, however, and leaves his lime bag in the hands of a young student: "He had spent so many years in executive positions that it seemed quite fitting that someone younger than himself, and less powerful in a worldly sense, should take over whatever was onerous in the work of the day." Habits do indeed die hard.

The important work that calls Taub is a meeting to reconsider the doubtful inclusion of the businessman in the experiment; Joe Lockman has already offended twice, once by carelessly leaving oil in the primitive kitchen stove so that it exploded and singed Katy's eyebrows when she came to light it, and again by playing a practical joke on Taub with the gun that Joe has brought along. But Utopia survives the test of Joe; he is not expelled, and the Utopians turn their attention to their plan to bring peace-loving Europeans to the United States to establish a "United States of Europe in Exile." They feel that solving the world's problems must start *somewhere*, but as tasks are assigned, individually they find excuses for it not to start with them.

On their property they are delighted to discover a field of wild strawberries, and they plan a picnic around the ripening of the berries. The dissolution of Utopia is prefigured in the events of the chosen day. A family appearing to be "of the very poorest farmer class" is seen picking the berries. Katy applies tact: "We don't mind your picking, but would you leave some of the strawberries for us?" The fact is that she *does* mind their picking, and she finds it inconceivable that they refuse to leave once she has politely pointed out that they are poaching. The encounter ends with the pickers making threatening gestures and shouting "obscene imprecations" as Katy retreats. She hastens home for help, but there her action, rather than that of the pickers, becomes the center of crisis. Some Utopians feel that she has done well, but others condemn her "individualistic conduct." As "all the latent hostilities of the past six weeks" come to the surface, Katy's husband and a veteran take Joe's gun and go to frighten the intruders away. When Joe appears on the scene, he is outraged that the people are being driven off, then even more outraged to realize that his *prop-*

erty—the gun—has been taken without his permission.

Utopia has run afoul of events for which it has no rules. But even if a rule is made to cover situations like this, "something else will come along, something we can't predict," and "the organism, unprepared, will react to it according to its own rules, the ones it was born with." When her property rights are challenged, Katy reverts to social prejudice, thinking frantically that "those brutal people . . . were incapable of appreciating the strawberries." Macdermott sees Lockman's hospitable reaction as "refreshing" until he recognizes that Lockman's horror is grounded in a "convention of the commercial world, where the handshake and the banner of welcome were axioms of intercourse"— the episode is bad PR. But however motivated, Joe's response still *looks* better than the unfriendly responses of the others. Macdermott does not know how he himself would have handled the pickers. "Morals to him were a chess problem in which the opening gambit elicited a set response, and the errors of modern society he laid simply to failure to use the unconventional opening advocated in his magazine's pages."

Katy muses, afterward, that the Utopians' problem is not to confuse "material triumphs with the triumph of . . . ideals." To Taub's objection that historically "man is shaped by his economy and his environment," she retorts, "Then let us get out of history." In history, Utopia will fail and fail again because people run true to form. Pretensions of moral superiority and rhetorical intellectualizing are no defense against the old Adam, who first tries saying "The strawberries are *mine*" and then proves it with a gun. Given a new Eden, we will always come to grief over the fruit.

There is nothing Edenic about the polder which is the setting of, much of *Cannibals and Missionaries.* For this novel, McCarthy assembles, once again, a

group, but this time her plot allows her to bring together people who in the normal course of events
would not seek each other out. The novel has been
called a *Canterbury Tales* with machine guns, and
there is some justice in the comparsion. McCarthy's
pilgrims number twenty-four, and they represent cler-
ical, legal, business, and educational callings; like
Chaucer's, they are portrayed with varying degrees of
sympathy.

The story of the chief hijacker, Jeroen, is tragic,
save in the fact that Jeroen's assault on the order of
things has no effect except pointless destruction; there
are no reverberations through the kingdom. McCarthy's
world is resistant to change, ineducable, and therefore
comic. The publication of this novel, with its improbable but possible act of terrorism, just a few weeks
before the seizing of American personnel in Iran seemed
a little eerie. Not that the events of recent history
parallel those of the novel, or that the novel prophesies
the international drama which began in November
1979, but there is enough of the fantastic in the behavior of Khomeini to make Jeroen's act seem less
incredible than it might have.

The original slate of hostages is a committee of
liberals en route to Iran to investigate the regime of
the Shah. The seizing of this "body of self-appointed
just men on an errand of mercy" is intended to strike
"at the core of the West's pious notion of itself." The
rationale is a little soft but not therefore unrealistic.
Terrorists are no more logical than the rest of us, and
Jeroen is an artist more interested in the form than in
the content of the enterprise. Originally the terrorists
—including besides the Dutch couple, Jeroen and his
girlfriend, Greet, two Germans, three Arabs, and a
South American—intended to seek permission to land
at an Arab airport, and the use of a farmhouse on a
new, sparsely populated polder in Holland was a back-

up plan. But as the details fell into place, Jeroen came to love the back-up plan and would have been disappointed had a sympathizing Arab nation let the plane land.

The title of the book refers to a game, or puzzle. Three cannibals and three missionaries want to cross a river. Their boat will hold only two people; the missionaries can row, and one cannibal can. The object is to devise a series of crossings by which all six can be moved without allowing cannibals at any time, on either side, to outnumber (and, of course, eat) the missionaries. The young Arab terrorist who solves the puzzle complains that the idea is racist since the real problem would be to prevent the missionaries from enslaving the cannibals. The puzzle posits an amiable relationship between cannibals and missionaries, aside from the premise that, outnumbered, the missionaries would be eaten. Just why they and the cannibals are fellow travelers is not at issue, and whether the hostages are cannibals or missionaries depends, doubtless, on the point of view. Ahmed's opinion is not without basis, to be sure, and some people might argue that the cannibals and missionaries deserve each other.

The novel begins by acquainting us with the Reverend Mr. Frank Barber, an Episcopal minister from New York, as he takes leave of his family. His narrative voice is the first and last we hear but only one of the many to be heard in the course of events; in this novel McCarthy uses the third-person technique she perfected in *The Group*, and the story is told in the manner of the characters, individually or in choruses. Approached by the Iranian student, Sadegh, Frank was inspired to participate in the mission by the example of the eighty-three-year-old Bishop, Augustus Hurlbut, his old friend and mentor. "The irony of it was that Gus . . . had not even been contacted, and

when the Iranians did get to him they used Frank's
name."

Always tolerant, Frank is not offended by this
deception, but the list of committee members as he
glimpses it from time to time seems to him "protean
in the extreme." Father Hesburgh's name disappears
and is replaced by that of Aileen Simmons, president
of Lucy Skinner, a women's college in Massachusetts.
Likewise, although the senatorial office remains represented, the name of the occupant changes. More important to Frank is the rabbi: "Is Rabbi Weill coming? Is it *definite*, Sadegh?" "Oh, yes, possible." "No,
not possible. *Sure*." "Yes, surely possible. Definite."
There has been nothing about a journalist, but by a
transmogrification the name "Weil" applies, finally,
to Sophie Weil, Jewish to be sure but a journalist and
not, as the others at first suppose, even the wife of the
rabbi. Frank regrets the definite absence of the rabbi,
and he wonders whether the group is "truly representative" since it does not include a black either.

During the first stage of the flight—New York to
Paris—Aileen's point of view dominates. Fifty and
single, Aileen is sorry to find Sophie among her companions. Aileen has designs on the Senator, but she
cannot compete with the younger woman. Sophie is
attractive, intelligent, and morally sensitive, in the
McCarthy tradition. Senator James Carey is widowed.
An extraordinarily eligible bachelor in his mid-fifties,
he resembles Eugene McCarthy in a limited way. He
was a leading Dove in opposition to the Vietnam War;
he had presidential aspirations which came to nothing;
and he is a poet, although unpublished. He is also per-
ceptive and level-headed, and he does not fall in love
with Sophie, or with Aileen. Completing the American group is a Middle East specialist from Buffalo,
Victor Lenz, ill-mannered and ill-groomed. When he

arrives at the airport, he is in need of a drink, which
the provident and saintly Bishop is able to provide
from his flask, ever-handy for medicinal purposes.
Victor is accompanied by his Persian cat, Sapphire,
who travels in her cage except when Victor foolishly
releases her and throws all of economy class into a
state of nerves.

In first class is the incomparable Charles Tennant, who has spotted his old friend, the Bishop, and
comes to economy to visit. He too is on the way to
Teheran. "On a *tour*. Can you imagine it? I'm part of
a first-class *package*." Charles' friends—"my million-
aries," he calls them, deploring their "Republican
sound and fury"—are a group of art collectors bent on
"discovering Iran as it threatened to make itself
scarce." Charles prefers the liberals and has to be sent
back to his own class when the stewardess clears the
aisle. Aileen, who prides herself on an active mind, is
left "pensive." As president of Lucy Skinner, she is
"concerned with gifts and bequests" and therefore
with the news of these collectors. She is also concerned with Charles. "Though he must be nearly
eighty and queer in every sense, there he was, a man
and unmarried. With a fair share of worldly goods."

In Paris, the committee is completed by the addition of an English historian, Archibald Cameron, and a
Dutch Member of Parliament, Henk Van Vliet de
Jonge. The Spanish monsignor does not appear. Cameron is not very talkative; he smokes a pipe and is
wont, "like a deity," to "disappear in a cloud of
smoke." Henk, however, talks a great deal. By virtue
of his interest in practical diplomacy and his fondness
for reasoning things out, he is to assume leadership
among the hostages. He and the Senator have a lot in
common, including elected political office and the
writing of poetry: Henk is a successful published

poet. The two men become very good friends. Henk and Sophie are to fall in love, but Henk is married.

When the hijackers make their move between Tel Aviv and Teheran, the passengers expect to be delayed, inconvenienced, ransomed, and then released. Cameron is moved to speech: "Rather a bore, this, don't you find? One reads about these bloody things but one doesn't expect them to happen to oneself." He has an alarming—from the point of view of de Jonge and Carey—instinct to resist the hijacking, but no opportunity presents itself. A tense moment is provided instead by Charles, who wants to join the liberals and brushes aside an Arab's gun with his cane: "Don't be frightened, my dear fellow. I have no intention of harming you. I have a long-standing sympathy with the Arab cause. . . ." He is allowed to pass, but just before the airplane lands—in Holland, to everybody's surprise—the drama assumes a grim tone. The hapless Sapphire, released again from her cage, is shot and killed by the hijackers.

After some time spent waiting on the ground, Aileen, who has rather a thing about first class, complains against the injustice that the millionaires may be freed and the committee held: "We have an important job to do, in Iran—doesn't anybody remember?—and they're just idle rich." She is untouched by Sophie's scorn of the idea of buying freedom at the expense of some "helpless fellow-mortals," but it is too late, in any case. She has been overheard.

When Henk is called to the cockpit for a conference with the terrorists, he is puzzled, but they want his advice. The Dutch refuse to provide the aircraft they demand. Henk counsels them to tell the Dutch minister, Den Uyl, that a Dutch parliamentarian is aboard and that therefore Dutch interests are involved; he is "crestfallen" to see that they will not

follow his advice. "No doubt it irked him as a lawyer
to give sound advice and perceive that it would not be
followed: he had begun to look on these malefactors
as his clients." It turns out that Holland does not have
the required aircraft, a helicopter large enough to
transport the hostages and the terrorists, and it has to
be borrowed, at some expense of national pride, from
neighboring fellow NATO member Germany. Reasoning from his knowledge of the helicopter's flying
range and landing capabilities, Henk knows before
they leave the Boeing that they will be going to the
New Polder, an area as yet sparsely inhabited because
recently reclaimed from the sea.

Before the transfer to the helicopter, the twelve
first-class hostages knew nothing of other hostages,
and they are not pleased to learn that "these people"
are included. Trying to puzzle out the reason for their
selection as "hostage material," they have already
thought anxiously of their treasures: "Helen's Vermeer. . . . And Harold's Cézannes. . . . Johnnie collected only sporting art, but his Stubbses and Degas
were worth fortunes, not to mention his Dufy sailing
subjects and his great Ward"—or Lily's watercolors.

The helicopter is set down on a deserted strip of
highway. By an oversight, it has skids rather than
wheels, and it will have to be pushed and pulled across
a small ditch and along a crude road to a farmer's barn,
where it can be concealed to prevent premature discovery. Millionaires, liberals, and terrorists accomplish
this difficult maneuver as a team. At one point, the
Senator seizes an ax and swings it authoritatively
through the underbrush where the Arab has been
hacking, but instantly the captors order him to put
down the potential deadly weapon. What has come
into play, Sophie thinks, is the "impulse to be helpful
common to most Americans. . . . it hurt the American
farm boy in [Carey] to watch somebody use an ax

that badly." When Ahmed cuts his thumb, the stewardess bandages it.

These little occurrences touched Sophie. Of course it was in the stewardess' training. And of course Ahmed was by way of becoming everybody's pet hijacker. But something more was at work, Sophie felt—an endearing, irrational, human tendency to make common cause.

The farmhouse to which the hostages are eventually taken has been stocked with food and wired with explosives; the owner and his family have been sent, by an elaborate scheme, on vacation at the hijackers' expense. The hostages settle quickly into a routine of watching television, playing games, and reading what little they have to read, including the committee's materials on the Shah's torture machinery. Meanwhile, the hijackers discover a need for education within their ranks. The Arabs are enchanted by the farmhouse. They suppose that the farmer must be an exploiter, and Greet, who does not believe in lying to the masses, attempts to make distinctions: the farmer uses machinery, not the labor of peasants, yet he is exploiting the "resources of the Third World, in his very tractor" and the fuel that runs it. By Dutch standards, this farmer is not very prosperous; an old Singer testifies to Greet that the wife economizes by making clothes for her family, "but in Yusuf's eyes, a sewing machine was a sign of affluence—another contradiction springing from historical unevenness." From the farmer's television, through Henk's translation, the hostages learn that there are four conditions for their release; a ransom of one and a quarter million dollars, the withdrawal of Holland from NATO and its breaking of relations with Israel, the release of "class-war" prisoners from Dutch jails (the absence of the rabbi undercut the intention of demanding release from Israeli prisons, to the disappointment of the Arab terrorists), and a helicopter to pick up some tape recordings. Jeroen intends to exchange the collectors for their works of art, and they will be required to make tapes giving instructions to their families. He reasons that although the lives of hostages have to be seen "in the perspective of the greater good for the greater number," works of art are "not to be touched with a ten-foot pole by any government respectful of 'values.'" People die in the course of nature, but works of art are "by their nature and in principle . . . imperishable. In addition, they were irreplaceable, which could not be said of their owners."

Only Helen refuses to make a tape, choosing death over the surrender of her Vermeer. She is not executed, however; her bathroom privilege is withdrawn. Alive, and with a stain on the back of her dress, Helen seems less heroic the next day. When her husband's toilet privilege is revoked, she makes the tape.

While the little colony awaits the arrival of the pictures, the Bishop dies of a stroke. The terrorists riddle the body with bullets and order it picked up by helicopter as evidence of their displeasure over the delay. For a time there is a good deal of activity at the farmhouse. As shipments of crated paintings are brought in, examined, and accepted in exchange for their owners, Carey, who perceived some time ago that Victor Lenz was working for the CIA and fears that the terrorists will reach the same conclusion, helps Lenz feign illness and get himself shipped out. Charles too gets sent away gratis, having convinced the terrorists that his porcelains are too fragile to be sent to the polder, but the incorrigible old subversive returns the next day, hitchhiking in the helicopter which brings an expert to testify to the authenticity of the Vermeer. He is firmly and finally sent away on the following day. At last only the terrorists and a "skeleton crew" of hostages remain in the farmhouse to wait; a month after the hijacking they are still waiting.

Henk assumes that the second demand, requiring a radical change in Holland's foreign policy, is *pro forma*, to satisfy the revolutionary image, and that the terrorists will settle for versions of the other three. Carey is the first to realize that Jeroen is "painting himself into a corner." By turning the farmhouse into a gallery, he has sought to make his position impregnable in order to force Den Uyl to accept the second demand. Both the Deputy and the Senator know that there can be no yielding that point by "the unbudging piece of Dutch reality represented by Mr. Owl."

Jeroen dislikes violence; he regrets the needless death of Sapphire. But his fellow terrorists feel that it is time to reinforce their demands by an execution. He and Greet call Henk in for the last of many conferences, and the outcome is that Henk makes a radio appeal to his government to grant the crucial demand. He knows that this will not affect the outcome. Regretfully, he explains again to Jeroen that Holland will not, indeed cannot, yield. Despondent, Jeroen sends them all—hostages and terrorists—for a walk. He wants to think. Only the devoted Ahmed, suspecting his intention, remains hidden in the house with him, but during the walk Greet has a sudden insight and brings the procession hastening back over protests— "Jeroen *said* we were to have thirty minutes"—just in time for Jeroen to cry furiously (in Dutch) "Get out!" before the house explodes.

Aileen and Frank have only "superficial cuts and bruises." Henk and Sophie live, but Henk is in a coma from a head injury for a time and Sophie loses her right arm. The others are dead and most of the paintings destroyed, sacrificed by Jeroen because he loved them. Flying together back to the United States, Aileen and Frank read a journal which Sophie kept and has given to Aileen. In it, she muses about art. What is its value, and to whom? And she ponders the hopeless plight of Jeroen. "I almost wish them [Jeroen and Greet] luck. Idealists, I know, are dangerous, but the claim of the ideal (Ibsen) has to be felt or else. . . . I w'd give an arm, as they say, if this thing could end grandly, the way Jeroen w'd wish, whatever that is by now."

"Chilling," as Aileen says. She and Frank are radically intact, and she knows it. "We were all changed, Aileen. Don't you sense it in yourself?" he earnestly insists. "No, I don't feel changed and, frankly, I don't notice any difference in you." Over his protests, she sums up. "We're two-dimensional, Reverend."

Art is central to McCarthy's design as to Jeroen's; it is both a subject of the novel and a device of the plot. Carey and Henk are poets. When Henk entertains the hijacked passengers by reciting from a prose poem by a Japanese writer, Carey completes the passage; it is a moment of recognition between the two. Not many people would know that passage, but Ahmed does. Overhearing, he "claims" the work on behalf of an imprisoned Japanese comrade who loved it. Henk muses that "if the youth was responsive to poetry, in principle he was salvageable," but he remembers, sadly, that some of the worst SS men were lovers of Rilke and Hölderlin. The idea of art in any form as a moral force is fallacious. "Living with beautiful things," as Charles says in his "fluting" voice, does not "rub off on" people.

But "claiming" the visual arts in one way or another engages most of the characters. The millionaires "own" great works of art. Eloise Chadwick knows the limitations of such ownership. Charles, she observes, owns everything he has seen, but if Chaddie loses his Cézannes, he has nothing. Frank (who unfortunately has no time to go to exhibitions) claims art for reli-

gion; Lenz claims it for politics. Aileen wants it for
her college's museum, the contents of which Charles
knows better than she does. Henk and Sophie, more
intellectual, are less partisan; theirs is the claim of appreciation. Carey knows less than they, and although
he examines the paintings with interest, he finds their
presence in the farmhouse disquieting. After it is
pointed out to him that an arm in a Cézanne is "out of
drawing," all he can see in the painting is the offend-
ing arm.

The hostages discuss art, seeking to define its uses,
and the voice of the Philistine is heard, most crudely
from Victor Lenz: "Why, Yusuf [an Arab terrorist]
here instinctively has a better appreciation of those
apples than all your museum boards. Cézanne painted
for *him*; he's been hungry and knows what an apple
means." (The essence of the apples, then, is their
juice; perhaps that is what Norine meant, all along.)
The discussions are recorded in Sophie's journal, along
with her musings on subjects which perplexed Peter
Levi. But Peter knew what art could do for him, and
Sophie is not so sure. It can develop taste, she decides,
but that boils down to teaching "the art of acquisition." The connoisseur is "merely a highly trained
consumer. . . . Art and wealth boon companions. Sad
but so." She doubts that an aesthete can be "a good
man." Art "excites cupidity, desire to possess," and
museums attract people who come to see the treasure.
Decentralization, she thinks, might be a partial solution; works of art, where possible, could "be returned
to point of origin." "Could Jeroen add it to demands?"
Although she notes that the idea is "whimsy," it is
revealing of an implicit if partial alliance with the terrorist.

The Vermeer—"Girl in a Blue Cap with a Guitar"
—is the most cherished of the paintings so improb-
ably uncrated and put on exhibit in the farmhouse

("Do have a look at the splendid Ward they have in
the next room," Charles urges). Henk and Sophie discuss it at length. "Vermeer, I think, Sophie, is always
painting time. . . . a split second of arrested motion."
Jeroen falls in love with it; as the days pass, he spends
more and more time sequestered with the painting,
and he sacrifices it, finally, because he loves it. Ahmed,
who briefly survives the explosion, attempts to make
Frank and Aileen understand that the sacrifice is "*le
geste sublime d'un grand révolutionnaire.*"

During his youth in Amsterdam, Jeroen wanted
to be an artist, "As though to pay back a debt he owed
for the joy his eyes were experiencing in the museums and along the canals." But when he became involved with his trade union and joined the Communist
Party, he came to hate art for art's sake and to consider it as useful only for "transmitting messages to the
people to incite them to action." Then he turned
against the Party as "merely another part of the system of world-wide oppression" and at last embraced
terrorism as "art for art's sake in the political realm."
A deed, he decided, is the only true work of art, with
"no aim outside itself." Trotsky was right in the idea
of permanent revolution. "Revolution . . . should mean
revolving, an eternal spinning, the opposite of evolu-
tion, so attractive to the bourgeois soul." The goal of
creating a just society may be an "impurity" in the
thought of a revolutionary. Jeroen comes full circle
when, in possession of the Vermeer, he loves the painting for its own sake and turns the act of terrorism into
a means to an end.

The trouble with terrorism, or any act, as art is
the temporal connection. A painting, a poem, a Gre-
cian urn can freeze a split second and render it eternal,
but a deed occurs in and flows with time; it has consequence. The moment passes—and it is only a moment
—when the sweep, the audacity, the *artistry* of the

thing are breathtaking. And then Jeroen is left with dwindling supplies, restless associates, and a useless assortment of lives and paintings. To prolong, to compromise, even to be freed to strike again and perpetuate the revolutionary spinning, no longer interest him. He has assailed the immovable object as an irresistible force. We do not need to see Jeroen's lifeless body to know that he has put up a stake.

NATO is not the point, nor is Holland's relationship with Israel. The novel does not discuss these institutions. To Jeroen, the NATO shield—displayed on a helicopter borrowed by Holland from Germany to "oblige a team of international terrorists"—serves to represent a "system of world-wide oppression," of which NATO members and the Soviet Union are equally culpable. By holding a group of "just men" and a house full of irreplaceable works of art, he challenges the West's commitment to human, material, and cultural values. The fundmental impurity of his sublime gesture, however, is its complicity in reducing art to currency. The Vermeer is the highest price he can imagine, but it is a price and it is turned down. Jeroen nets no more than any ordinary hijacker.

Social change does not follow from even the boldest and most imaginative act of terrorism, but neither does it seem to follow from the orderly use of existing machinery within the system. The mission to Iran is moot. Sophie calls it, perhaps ironically, interference in the internal affairs of another country. Henk considers the Shah an "easy target," being neither friend nor foe; one would be embarrassed to expose a friend, but one might be refused admittance by a foe. The committee might have succeeded in making its report, but whether it could have effected the cessation of alleged violations of human rights is another matter. It was, nonetheless, a modest plan, reasonable and humane, surely an admirable form of po-

litical action despite the mixed motives of the liberals,
the slapdash planning, and the sinister presence of the
CIA. In his official capacity, the Senator has had a long
career of "bucking the system" at home, but his as-
sessment of his accomplishments is disheartening.
When Henk tells Jeroen that his demands will not be
met "unless many facts change and evolve, of their
own weight, independently," he voices a principle
which applies as well to the efforts of an elected official working within the established order. Most dur-
able of the birds in the novel is Mr. Owl, embodiment
of the imperviousness of human institutions.

There are other birds which serve the peripheral
theme of man at odds with nature. Frank's binoculars
come in handy for viewing the birds on the polder,
which exists by man's reduction of nature. His son
sent the binoculars along because he read in the 1913
Britannica that Iran offers four hundred species of
birds for viewing. To be sure, that edition predates the
development of Iran's petroleum industry, which may
have reduced the bird population; like much about
Frank, the encyclopedia is an unreliable witness in the
modern world. The hostages do not need binoculars to
see the buzzards hovering above the Bishop when he is
bagged and waiting in the field; Ahmed valiantly
fights them off until the arrival of that more formida-
ble scavenger, the helicopter.

As they bless the terrorist for driving away the
buzzards, the hostages watching from the farmhouse
window forget that, except for Ahmed and his like,
the Bishop would not be awaiting pickup in such an
unseemly manner. So much depends upon the point of
view. Birds are seen through binoculars, pictures by
the wrong light, the Dutch government—and NATO
and Israel—from a "weensy change in perspective,"
as Charles says. Allegations against the Shah are im-
material to the Arabs, whose interest lies with their

comrades in Israeli jails. NATO is a shield to its member nations but an agent of exploitation to the terrorists.

And if the Bishop had not so providentially died, the terrorists might have shot their bullets into a living hostage. Carey considers the old Bishop a good man, and nothing in the novel gainsays it. Intimate with God, as the earnestly religious Frank is not, he is also more at ease in the world. His flask does more than Frank's exhortations to calm the hostages. He is as guiltless as Sapphire—"She gave her life for us," sobs Aileen, who does not like cats, on the occasion of her death—and perhaps both die for the sins of others, or at least for the sin of bringing them along, but there is no redemption, only loss. The Bishop misplaces his faith in the course of his mental wanderings during the night of his death, and we can only hope, with Lily, that sometime during "the watches of the night" he found it again.

Although some of the hostages come to terms with the point of view of their captors, there is no seduction or brainwashing by the terrorists. They are impersonal and businesslike, except for Ahmed, who is sociable and well disposed toward the prisoners. Jeroen and Greet gradually relax toward Henk. In handling the domestic affairs of the hostages, Greet is harsh but not pointlessly cruel. There are only traces of the childlike dependence that hostages often develop; and although Beryl's ridiculous courtship of Ahmed is true to the patterns of hostage psychology, one suspects that Beryl would flirt with Ahmed anywhere she met him.

The hostages are cooperative because resistance would be fatal and because of the tendency that Sophie noted to make common cause. Actually, a common cause is built into the plan: the freeing of the hostages. Archie Cameron is an irrepressible sub-

versive, seeing a "duty to resist," keeping an eye out
for opportunity, finally smuggling a sketch of a "prac-
ticable tunnel" out under Eloise Chadwick's powder
puff. Victor Lenz, nervous about his double role,
contemplates defection, but poor Victor is not very
bright. He earnestly assures Carey that his CIA connection could not have hurt the work of the committee, but Victor is all sentiment and dependency, as his
unwise inclusion of Sapphire among the liberals at-
tests. Out of compassion and a sense of responsibility,
the Senator undertakes the subversive act of getting
Lenz sent away.

The underground of resistance is very small indeed. In general, the force of habit works to make the
artificial world in the farmhouse parallel the real. The
hostages get rather smelly and disheveled, unwashed
and wearing always the same clothes; and they are
surprised to find how interesting it is to have leisure
time. But Frank carries out his pastoral mission, playing hymns on the harmonium, practicing tolerance,
inspiring, or trying to inspire, his companions, and,
when it is necessary, conducting a primitive funeral
service for his old friend the Bishop. Meanwhile
Sophie, a journalist, keeps a journal. Denise, a stewardess, prepares and serves the meals. The citizens carry
on under the hostile government. They even petition
it about the sleeping arrangments, with apparently
some notion that a majority appeal to "humane" considerations should have some clout even here, and Aileen wants a suggestion box (though one does not
know whether she is serious about that).

Besides the millionaires' masterpeices, the hostages
have little at stake except their lives. Their property
and convictions do not count. But still they are surprised at how vulnerable opinions are. It is Charles,
"being dreadful," who articulates the process by
which they can shift.

It was that interesting third demand that brought it home
to me. Why, my dear, I said to myself, if the whole criminal population of Holland were turned loose . . . I'd have
no objection as long as it meant that I'd be allowed to
journey to Naqsh-i-Rustan with my ears and toes and
fingers still safely about me. . . . I found myself led to
question the social utility of prisons. . . . And . . . can we
honestly say that it would be a tragedy if Holland were
to leave NATO and suspend relations with Israel? My own
answer, I admit, would be prejudiced. As a pacifist, I hold
no brief for NATO, and, though I'm not unsympathetic
to Israel, I feel she could use a little lesson.

The intellect is no ally of the conscience, however, as Carey well knows. Recognizing the futility of
the love between Henk and Sophie, he thinks briefly
of marrying Sophie when they are released, as a
"proof of loyalty to Henk" and a way to "cement this
experience." But he gives more serious thought to
Lily, nearer his age and better suited to the role of his
wife. Carey's life is a continuum, and this experience is
part of it. Although, like Henk, he from the beginning
recognizes his responsibility for leadership, he cannot
see what to do beyond "vetoing hare-brained counter-
insurgency schemes" and setting the tone. Carey's
manner is detached and playful; his besetting sin is
pride. He is Catholic and does not expect much of
humanity; God is "the only person" to whom he can
talk and who can anger him. Whereas Henk first re-
acts to the hijacking with vexation and mystification
about the who and why of it, Carey casts about ironically for "a principle . . . in this affair that a righteous
man might be inclined to do battle for." He is "unhappy" about the hijacking because there is "no con-
stitutional or democratic reply" to it. Intellectually as
well as "in his gut" he believes that force should be
resisted, but he can see no reasonable way to resist.

Later, anticipating an "invitation" to appeal to the

Dutch to yield on the second demand, he reflects that for a liberal, "to be instrumental in the dismantling of NATO and the ostracism of Israel would be a torture worthy of SAVAK [the Shah's police]." But like Henk, he knows that the appeal would not affect the outcome.

So then? . . . He might allow himself to do a distasteful, base thing secure in the private knowledge that it could have no effect. The operative word was "base." It was an ordinary matter of honor.

He is not called upon to make an appeal, but he knows that "the easiest thing to do" would be to make it. He is "wary" of his intellect, which can readily support a dishonorable action by showing him the futility of refusal.

Carey does not come to admire or sympathize with the terrorists as Henk and Sophie do, but he is interested in the tacit acknowledgment that he and Henk are their peers; he believes that terrorism is an "unprofitable exercise of juvenile energy and imagination." The terrorist, limited by the "*status quo ante* that he was setting out to topple,*" accomplishes nothing. The thought leads the Senator to review his own career:

A few immediate gains compatible with the *status quo ante* and no fundamental change. He could claim the fall of Johnson and the tempering of the war in Vietnam. But the fall of Johnson had eventuated in Nixon (which had to figure as a debit), and the war in Vietnam would have been winding down anyway. . . . Observing that, he laughed, feeling a real fondness for Jeroen. What Greet liked to call the armed politics of the underground—their euphemism, he guessed, for terror—was only the kid brother of minority electoral politics, with the same old Achilles' heel.

Carey is not, however, morally liberated by recognition of his ineffectuality.

Henk, also a "political animal," finds a natural place in the center of the action. He knows what a polder is and can tell the hostages where they are. He is a member of the Dutch government and can interpret it for the terrorists. He knows the Dutch language and can translate the television announcements for the English-speaking hostages. He even exercises a modicum of power in mediating between captors and hostages. He takes the terrorists as "clients," advising and explaining and finally joining them in an appeal to his government. Telling Jeroen that this is no battle of wills—"It is your single will against the inertia of facts"—he feels "compunction" for the terrorist. "If finally he was convincing him, brute force of reason was killing a long-held dream. He was sorry for that: it would have been wonderful if the brave fellow, single-handed and by sheer persistence, could have taken the Lowlands out of NATO." What Henk regrets, after the explosion, is that he deprived Jeroen of hope. "He had let his love of reasoning carry him away" and told Jeroen the truth, which made him despair.

"That's crazy," Aileen objects later to Frank. "You have to take hope away from dangerous criminals, show them they can't win, don't you?" But to Henk, it is all an intellectual exercise, like cannibals and missionaries, to be worked out on a level somewhere above the inertia of facts. Although he is sympathetic toward Jeroen, and although he loves Sophie enough to die for her, he does not quarrel with *status quo* in his government and in his family. Henk acknowledges in himself a certain "levity of commitment" which is evident in his ability to transfer his political function to the terrorists' party and carry on, out of an impulse something like Carey's in seizing Ahmed's ax: he hates to see the thing done badly. But Henk's use of his talents has moral implications.

Early in the hijacking, he does not want to "appear as privy counselor to a ruthless gang of terrorists," but "appear" is the key word; he is willing to *be* their counselor, for "no lives depended on his decisions. Ideally irresponsible, a captured pawn, he could only muse and conjecture." Grandson of a popular novelist, himself a successful poet, Henk operates on a fictive plane. He enjoys a fantasy that Holland is an imaginary country with a secret language, a poetic conceit which frames his surprise to overhear the Dutch language spoken outside of Holland by the couple who turn out to be terrorists. Early in his captivity he feels that his wife and children, "dear vested interests," are remote; and, much later, when the opportunity is offered, he cannot think of a message to send them. He is capable of suspending contact with one imaginary world to carry on in another, for he has no footing in either. When his intellect counsels him to appeal to his government because his doing so will have no effect, he makes a credible, but not especially creditable, response.

Aileen is perplexed about Henk's sympathy for the terrorists as she and Frank discuss their adventure on the way home. Aileen is not so tolerant or kindly as Frank, but she tries to be good. Her candor is one of her better qualities when it is not one of her worst. "But, Aileen, surely you feel sorrow," Frank persists after she has denied having been changed by their experience. "Not much. Only superficially, like with our cuts. Yet you could say"—she laughs—"that I lost two matrimonial prospects in the great explosion." She added Archie to her list after discovering that he was widowed.

Aileen's chief preoccupation, other than matrimony, is a rigid sense of fairness, which usually strengthens her sense of her own importance. She frets about who is served first, and why; she resents first class; she is irritated when the hijacked plane circles before landing in Schiphol: "Wouldn't you think that at least we'd have priority?" When a rivalry develops between liberals and millionaires over which group was the primary target of the terrorists, Aileen is naturally the one who argues the point with Potter. "Assuming you were a terrorist," he asks her, "would you hold *you* for ransom or my wife? I've no doubt that you have many fine qualities that make you valuable to your associates, whatever you do in life, but let me state it bluntly: what do you *own*?" One might think that Potter dserves whatever he gets for putting it quite *this* bluntly, but perhaps not.

. . . I'm a *public person*, Mister Potter. You don't know what that means. Why, right this minute, I'll bet, my picture is on the front page of the *Times*. . . . You can't say that for your wife and her friends. They'll be lucky if their picture is in the society columns, which have blacks and Jews nowadays, in case you didn't know it. I'm sorry, Mister Potter, but you don't *mean* anything in the world. And nobody is more on to that than a terrorist.

As irritating as anything else about Aileen is the fact that she is often right, or nearly so. Henk expresses a similar idea by the analogy of the Soviet labor camp. "The common-law criminals—murders, thieves, and such—would be serving short sentences, while the political offenders would be in for long stretches." The millionaires merely profit by the social structure; the liberals bolster it ideologically. But Aileen is not a liberal. Although she supports certified liberal causes, she knows what she knows, and what she does not know she does not learn. She is inaccessible.

So is Frank. Since he considers himself an idealist, Frank is interested in Sophie's opinion that idealists are dangerous. But she refers to Jeroen; the word has to be stretched out of shape to cover Frank as well. He is a reductive kind of "idealist" who confuses ideals with platitudes and charges through life finding good in everything. His childlike wonder, his folksy idiom, his downright sincerity (Frank-ness) would be as tedious in life as they are gratifyingly authentic in fiction. Mentally rehearsing a sermon to justify his mission to Iran, he presses into service the story of Jonah to illustrate the "divine call to betake ourselves to a place far from home," and the ministry of Jesus to show the validity of action in the secular realm: Jesus "does not offer any *spiritual* comfort, any pie in the sky, to the leper—he cures the man and sends him on his way."

Working out the details will be difficult—he wrestles with the Jonah story throughout the novel—but Frank "never let details get between him and a powerful idea." His ideas come to him ready-made in exhortatory preacherly rhetoric. He instructs his fellow hostages to look on their plight as "a call. A call to deepen our faith and our brotherly love. . . . To extend our experience. . . . Not everyone has the good fortune—yes, the good fortune—to be hijacked." At the end, watching the movie on the airplane without earphones, he and Aileen follow the story quite well; they are used to watching television in Dutch, which they do not understand. "It had been good mental training, the Reverend Frank acknowledged, glad to be reminded of the need to count their rewards." But the good Reverend follows neither words nor pictures; he has no internal mechanism for interpreting information.

These two voices, Aileen's and Frank's, insistent throughout, continue to talk through the final page and into eternity. They are part of what perdures, or remains. So are the millionaires. The comic characters are numerous and deftly drawn, like Beryl, the "overweight child in her late thirties" still rebelling against

Lily, her dreamy mother; and like Chadwick, with his faith that he can barter his Cézannes for his freedom without losing them because his lawyer—or the FBI or the Treasury Department—will see to it. But we need not apply the "death as symbol of mortality" principle across the board; in an explosion there are random victims and survivors, and there are injuries. Henk and Sophie are injured in parts instrumental to their professions, but Henk suffers no permanent brain damage and Sophie can get an artificial arm and a one-handed typewriter. Not unchanged, they can go on. Carey is the only one among the liberals who cannot resume his former life. "He had so much to give," Frank says regretfully. "He'd given it," Aileen replies. "That page had already turned."

Cannibals and Missionaries is moderately long—369 pages—and it has a complex plot and a large cast of characters. It is well proportioned, and the essential parts—beginning, middle, end—are well defined; it is, as one reviewer said, a very "shapely" novel. With her usual meticulousness, McCarthy controls her materials. There are twenty-four hostages and eight terrorists, and she knows them; she knows where they are and what they are doing. Although one readily forgives a novelist like Faulkner, who now and then forgets a character's name and assigns him a new one, or shows at the end of a novel the destruction by fire of a wooden house that in the middle of the novel was built of bricks, a very minor but distinct source of pleasure in reading McCarthy's novels is that she does *not* commit these small errors.

In "The Fact in Fiction," McCarthy speaks of the continuity of a novel with real life, and nowhere is the quality better demonstrated than in *Cannibals and Missionaries*. As always, McCarthy writes from a thorough knowledge of her factual as well as fictional subject matter. In the introductory acknowledgments

to the novel, she mentions some of the kinds of assistance she needed in describing the polder and the
Dutch farmer's house. We can depend on the accuracy of the lessons in geography and sociology that
are a peripheral benefit of reading the book. And I do
not know whether thirty-two people have ever been
obliged to move a helicopter on skids, using frozen
mud as a lubricant, but having read *Cannibals and Missionaries* I am fairly sure that it could be done.

McCarthy's characters are citizens of the contemporary world. James Carey thinks affectionately of
his "only friend in the Senate, old Sam Ervin (now,
alas, retired)" and remarks to Aileen, about his non-
candidacy in the 1972 presidential election, that "Anyway, Nixon would have clobbered me. I would have
rather it happened to George." We know that it did
happen to George (McGovern); we may not as easily
recall that James Carey lost the nomination to him.
Den Uyl was the real-life Prime Minister of Holland
for a time; McCarthy had dinner with him when she
was working on the book in which he figures, off-
stage, as an "unbudging piece of Dutch reality." And
so when we hear that Father Hesburgh did not join
the committee but Aileen Simmons did, we have an
impulse to look her up in *Who's Who*. We are interested to know, as Lily is, whether the terrorist named
Carlos is *the* Carlos, and perhaps a little disappointed,
as she is, to learn that he is not.

Naturally a Plains Democrat of liberal persua-
sions, like James Carey, would have known the ironic
Shakespeare-quoting Senator from North Carolina and
would have liked him; from *The Mask of State*, dedi-
cated to the Honorable Sam J. Ervin, Jr. ". . . with
russet yeas and honest kersey noes," we know that
McCarthy liked him, too. *Cannibals and Missionaries*
will require copious footnoting when recent memory

becomes modern history. But the impact of the novel is not dependent upon knowledge of persons and events or even of acceptable political opinions. One knows that McCarthy, like Charles Tennant, holds no brief for the West, and that she herself lives in France, which pulled out of NATO in the sixties.

The comfortable familiarity of the political terrain is merely a setting; the psychological terrain, also familiar but not always comfortably so, is the point of interest. Human nature can be appalling. When the hostages decide that Jeroen is "loath," at least, to take human life, a fact that should be "cause for rejoicing," they react with more complex emotions to this alteration of their satisfactory "image" of him:

He seemed so hard and resolute, yet fair in his own way—an enemy one could respect. And since one was in his power anyway, it was preferable to look up to him. As Margaret said, a Jeroen who was "loath" to take human life was too small for his boots.

But in what way is kidnaping fair? And from what stature does one "look up to" a killer? Yet we are familiar with the attitude; we may even be caught off guard and nod agreeably—of what earthly use is a humane terrorist? These are highly civilized people, yet when they are not expressing the "warrior" values —as Henk says—of their class, they are often arguing with each other about who is more important to the terrorists. Human nature can also be very trivial.

The other side of that coin might be that human nature can be grand, but McCarthy seems not to think so. Decency seems to be the upper limit of human possibility—or, to elaborate, the practice of solid virtues like honor, compassion, sacrifice, and truthfulness. A trim reckoning, but no mean achievement on the personal level. On a larger scale, McCarthy does not

offer much hope, but then we do not read her for
reassurance.

McCarthy's latest two novels have international
settings. Her physical absence from America is partly
responsible for her moving her fiction to Europe; the
American voices she hears are the voices of Americans
abroad, and McCarthy always writes from observation.

Cannibals and Missionaries is susceptible to the
recurring criticism that McCarthy is more essayist
than novelist. One reader wonders why she wrote this
book as a novel; another finds the long periods of in-
action tedious. We may again pass over the question
of genre. As the term is commonly used, *Cannibals
and Missionaries* is a novel. But to say so does not clear
it of the charge that it contains so many monologues,
both internal and external, that the subjects of conversations and reflections, rather than action and character, sometimes dominate our attention.

There is, to be sure, a lot of talk in *Ulysses*, *The
Sound and the Fury*, and *Portnoy's Complaint*. But
McCarthy's fiction hardly resembles Joyce's, or Faulkner's, or Roth's. Although she exposes the minds and
actions of her characters, she does not often explore
their souls and invite us to *feel* with them. Indeed, we
hardly even mourn their deaths—fortunately, since
their mortality rate is appalling. We like many of
them, but amusement and embarrassment are the emotions we are most likely to feel on their behalf; and we
do not willingly identify with most of them. We do,
however, judge them. We think about them in terms
of what they do and ought to do, not of how they feel
or why they feel that way. Our attention is directed
to how their minds work, what they know, and how
they explain themselves. McCarthy believes (as she
says in the interview with Niebuhr) that truth is
knowable; her characters are prone to err, but not

with impunity and not without presenting their case.
They argue and rationalize. They think in essays;
sometimes they write letters and journals. And finally,
we cannot believe that Sophie's journal entries and
Pete Levi's letter are written to portray Sophie and
Peter; rather, these characters seem at times to have
been created to ponder ideas.

If a weakness of McCarthy's fiction is its essayis-
tic tendencies, its great strength is the accuracy with
which she portrays characters, particularly comic
characters, giving new life and individuality to universal types. Aileen Simmons belongs to the tradition of
the Wife of Bath, going on a pilgrimage and looking
for a mate, gregarious, a little overdressed, outspoken,
ever-mindful of precedence. Her eye is on the clerkly
Senator, an unlikely prospect if ever there was one,
but she also contemplates a rich old man, Charles Tennant; like Allison of Bath, she is alert to any opportunity. Frank Barber has literary kinsmen in Parson
Adams and Pangloss and, doubtless, some Ur-Parson
among the cavemen. Of more recent vintage is the
wicked Charles, genuinely liberal, dauntless, and dreadful in his confessions of the human frailties that plague
us all. He is a comic character and a homosexual, and
the two facts have nothing to do with each other; the
gay Charles is offered as character without any statement about his sexual identity, which is a problem
only to Aileen. At eighty, he is in any case past his
prime, but he is physically fearless and a good foil to
the other men with their macho instincts.

McCarthy is generous with physical descriptions
of her characters, but often a single feature or gesture
is emphasized by repetition until it has almost the
effect of caricature: the Senator is tall and has a "mag-
nificent" head of white hair, Dottie (*The Group*) has
a nervous little cough, and so on. All her characters
exist in a world of physical *things*; the essentials of

life, food, clothing, and shelter, are abundantly described.

In "Settling the Colonel's Hash," McCarthy
makes the point that "all human actions are symbolic
because they represent the person who does them."
Only in that sense are the colonel's hash and her own
sandwich symbolic: "they typify the colonel's food
tastes and mine." Peter Levi practices his mother's
principle of always including something good to eat in
stories told to children. McCarthy nearly always includes something to eat in her stories. Mulcahy licking
his ice-cream spoon; Domna eating her nightly meal of
an apple, cheese, salami, a roll; and Alma cooking her
single chop and bright green peas are natural allegories
of self-indulgence, austerity, and self-discipline. Simi-
larly, clothing and housing serve to identify characters. They show up for weddings, funerals, court
hearings, and journeys dressed in the wrong things, or
borrowed things, or the right things. Ironing boards
and needles appear to keep clothes in good repair, or
else they get wrinkles and rips, which are duly noted.
Places of residence express character, even of the absent
Dutch family whose pot plants Greet wants to let die
for lack of water as a political gesture and Lily waters
as a matter of simple conservation.

But the most telling means of characterization in
McCarthy's fiction is the voices. Her ear is faultless.
She can condense a personality into a phrase, or she
can sustain a character's rhythms and idioms through
an entire book. Snatches of casual dialogue epitomize a
type: "But of course one can't trust him, that's the
whole beauty of him," cries Cathy of Furness (*The
Groves of Academe*). Whether she is rendering life
faithfully or descending upon it with a "swerve and
swoop,"[2] McCarthy's voices ring true. She herself
mourns the loss of the authorial voice in fiction and

has said that she wants to restore it; she enjoyed writing the Venice and Florence books because in them she spoke with her own voice. But in her fiction she continues to use the voices of her characters, and her readers can only rejoice, for in the creation of voices she is unequaled. She calls her technique "ventriloquism," but the term, which she uses repeatedly and which, naturally, is echoed by her critics, seems unfortunately chosen. The ventriloquist and his dummy speak *for* each other, and the dummy has no voice. But with Mary McCarthy's characters, who are not dummies, one has the sense not that she makes them talk but that she hears them talking. The difference is considerable.

There remains much to be said about McCarthy as artist. Her novels are among the best of our time, but although they are hailed as events when they appear, they soon drop out of sight; only *The Groves of Academe* and *The Oasis* are well established as classics. There will be assessments and reassessments; the novels have lasting artistic value and are worth discussing. McCarthy has a way of getting to the heart of the matter about liberals concerned with personal or national morality, the balance of nature, social amelioration, and other high-minded ideas. She writes less about our admirable ideals, which stand alone, than about our wobbly conduct. We often take offense; if we mean well, and if we are right, we do not like to have our self-deceptions and ineffectual methods pointed out. We feel that being right is enough. The trouble with Mary McCarthy is that she does not, and she often makes us look less than heroic.

I have applied the word "satire" sparingly, partly out of reluctance to use it without a definition but also because McCarthy is not chiefly a satirist. Her characters are too warmly individualized to be satiric. There

are exceptions, but in general her characters are comic
—like Warren Coe at times absurd, but redeemed by
authorial grace. Humor is a healthier corrective device
than scorn, if one can laugh at oneself. The objects of
her satire are more likely to be ideas or institutions:
Freudian psychology run roughshod over simple
human emotions, educational theories applied despite
their documented failure.

Criticism of McCarthy is often cantankerous and
given to condescension or sarcasm. She has, however,
inspired some very thoughtful sympathetic criticism,
most notably by Irvin Stock, Elizabeth Hardwick,
Doris Grumbach, and Barbara McKenzie. She rarely
inspires indifference. She has enjoyed some degree of
prominence throughout her adult life, based on admiration and terror among the literary few at first and
then, later, on the popularity of *The Group*, which
must regretfully be attributed in part to sensational-
ism. But her niche in American letters has not yet
been defined. Her work is, we may hope, not yet
complete.

Her most recent novel is evidence, according to
Time's reviewer, that Mary McCarthy has not mel-
lowed. In speaking the truth, she often offends those
of us who enjoy the carefully framed view from our
positions—right or left, passé or avant-garde—for as
she sees it, truth is not so neatly enclosed. She is at
times distressingly impartial. She has kept the habit of
her childhood of seeing both sides, an admirable habit;
and she very often whirls and attacks *us*, the well-
meaning readers, for our self-deceptions and our
choices of the easy way out.

Although McCarthy is no longer interested in the
quest for self—she says that the self must be made, not
found—she need not repudiate the early heroine, for
she, too, strains to perceive truth by which to live—in
marriage, in career, in America. No moral vision can

come from deception, and therefore McCarthy believes that "to vow to tell the truth, whether pleasing
to the authorities or to your readers, is genuine literary commitment. I myself do not know of any other
kind."

Notes

1. BIOGRAPHY

1. Elaine Showalter, "Killing the Angel in the House: The Autonomy of Women Writers," p. 346.
2. Brock Brower, "Mary McCarthyism," p. 68.
3. Ibid., p. 65.
4. Ibid., p. 62.
5. Mary McCarthy, in an interview with Elisabeth Niebuhr, "The Art of Fiction XXVII," p. 72.
6. Brower, p. 64.
7. Niebuhr, p. 66.
8. Doris Grumbach, *The Company She Kept*, p. 180.
9. Ibid., p. 194.
10. Ibid., p. 195.
11. Ibid., p. 193.
12. Brower, p. 65.

2. *Memories of a Catholic Girlhood:* THE AUTHOR'S EARLY YEARS

1. Eleanor Widmer, "Finally a Lady: Mary McCarthy," p. 95.

3. "PRESERVE ME IN DISUNITY:" THE QUEST FOR IDENTITY IN *The Company She Keeps*

1. Elisabeth Niebuhr, "The Art of Fiction XXVII," p. 66.
2. Louis Auchincloss, "Mary McCarthy," p. 176.
3. Irvin Stock, *Mary McCarthy*, p. 28.

4. THE DEMANDS OF THE ETHICAL AND THE QUEST FOR SUPERIORITY IN *A Charmed Life*

1. Elisabeth Niebuhr, "The Art of Fiction XXVII," p. 86.
2. Irvin Stock, *Mary McCarthy*, p. 28.

5. A BRAVE NEW GENERATION: *The Group*

1. Doris Grumbach, *The Company She Kept*, p. 192.
2. Irvin Stock, *Mary McCarthy*, p. 9.
3. Ruth Mathewson, "The Vassar Joke," p. 13.
4. Ibid., p. 14.
5. Norman Mailer, "The Case against McCarthy: A Review of *The Group*," p. 137.

6. A SCHOLARLY MAZE AND A QUESTION OF JUSTICE: *The Groves of Academe*

1. Ruth Mathewson, "The Vassar Joke," p. 14.

7. THE LIBERAL IMAGINATION AND THE MODERN DILEMMA: *Birds of America*

1. Voltaire, *Candide, or Optimism*. Robert M. Adams trans. and ed., p. 77.

8. THE AUTHOR IN HER OWN VOICE: ESSAYS ON DIVERSE SUBJECTS

1. Alfred Kazin, *Bright Book of Life*, p. 188.

9.   THE SONS OF ADAM IN AND OUT OF EDEN:
The Oasis and *Cannibals and Missionaries*

1.   Doris Grumbach, *The Company She Kept*, p. 137.
2.   Elisabeth Niebuhr, "The Art of Fiction XXVII,"
     p. 89.

Bibliography

1. WORKS BY MARY MCCARTHY

The Company She Keeps. New York: Simon and Schuster, 1942.

The Oasis. New York: Random House, 1949.

Cast a Cold Eye. New York: Harcourt, Brace, and World, 1950.

The Groves of Academe. New York: Harcourt, Brace, and World, 1952.

A Charmed Life. Harcourt, Brace, and World, 1955.

Sights and Spectacles: 1937–1956. New York: Farrar, Straus, and Company, 1956.

Venice Observed. New York: Reynal and Company, 1956.

Memories of a Catholic Girlhood. New York: Harcourt, Brace, and World, 1957.

The Stones of Florence. New York: Harcourt, Brace, and World, 1959.

On the Contrary: Articles of Belief, 1946–1961. New York: Farrar, Straus, and Company, 1962.

The Group. New York: Harcourt, Brace, and World, 1963.

Mary McCarthy's Theatre Chronicles, 1937–1962. New York: Farrar, Straus, and Company, 1963.

Vietnam. New York: Harcourt, Brace, and World, 1967.

Hanoi. New York: Harcourt, Brace, and World, 1968.

The Writing on the Wall, and Other Literary Essays. New York: Harcourt, Brace, and World, 1970.

Birds of America. New York: Harcourt, Brace, Jovanovich, 1971.

Medina. New York: Harcourt, Brace, Jovanovich, 1972.

The Mask of State: Watergate Portraits. New York: Harcourt, Brace, Jovanovich, 1974.

The Seventeenth Degree: How It Went, Vietnam, Hanoi,

Medina, Sons of the Morning. New York: Harcourt,
Brace, Jovanovich, 1974.

Cannibals and Missionaries. New York: Harcourt, Brace,
Jovanovich, 1979.

Ideas and the Novel. New York: Harcourt, Brace, Jovanovich, 1980.

2.   WORKS ABOUT MARY MCCARTHY

Auchincloss, Louis. "Mary McCarthy." *In Pioneers and
Caretakers: A Study of Nine American Women Novelists.* Minneapolis: University of Minnesota Press,
1965.

Brower, Brock. "Mary McCarthyism." *Esquire,* July 1962,
pp. 62–67, 113.

Chamberlain, John. "The Novels of Mary McCarthy." In
The Creative Present, Nona Balakian and Charles
Simmons, eds. New York: Doubleday, 1963.

Enright, D. J. "Contrary Wise: The Writings of Mary
McCarthy." In *Conspirators and Poets.* London:
Chatto and Windus, 1966.

Goldman, Sherli. *Mary McCarthy: A Bibliography.* New
York: Harcourt, Brace, and World, 1968.

Gottfried, Alex, and Sue Davidson. "Utopia's Children: An
Interpretation of Three Political Novels." *The Western Political Quarterly,* March 1962, pp. 17–32.

Grumbach, Doris. *The Company She Kept.* New York:
Coward-McCann, 1967.

Hardwick, Elizabeth. "Mary McCarthy." In *A View of
My Own.* New York: Noonday Press, 1963.

Kazin, Alfred. *Bright Book of Life.* Boston: Little, Brown,
and Company, 1973.

Mailer, Norman. "The Case against McCarthy: A Review
of *The Group.*" In *Cannibals and Christians.* New
York: Dial Press, 1966.

Mathewson, Ruth. "The Vassar Joke." *Columbia University Forum* VI (1963), iv, 10–16.

McKenzie, Barbara. *Mary McCarthy.* New York:
Twayne, 1966.

Niebuhr, Elisabeth. "The Art of Fiction XXVII." *The Paris Review*, Winter-Spring 1962, pp. 58–94.

Schlueter, Paul. "The Dissections of Mary McCarthy." In *Contemporary American Novelists*, Harry T. Moore, ed. Carbondale: Southern Illinois University Press, 1964.

Showalter, Elaine. "Killing the Angel in the House: The Autonomy of Women Writers." *Antioch Review* 32 (1973), 339–353.

Stock, Irvin. *Mary McCarthy*. Minneapolis: University of Minnesota Press, 1968.

Stock Irvin. "Mary McCarthy." In *American Writers: A Collection of Literary Biographies* II, Leonard Unger, ed. New York: Charles Scribner's Sons, 1974.

Taylor, Gordon. "Cast a Cold 'I': Mary McCarthy on Vietnam." *Journal of American Studies* 9 (1975), 103–114.

Widmer, Eleanor. "Finally a Lady: Mary McCarthy." In *The Fifties: Fiction, Poetry, Drama*, Warren French, ed. Deland, Florida: Everett/Edwards, 1970.

Index

MODERN LITERATURE SERIES

In the same series (continued from page ii)